Creating Winning Classrooms

PETER HOOK AND ANDY VASS

David Fulton Publishers
London

David Fulton Publishers Ltd
Ormond House, 26–27 Boswell Street, London WC1N 3JD

www.fultonpublishers.co.uk

First published in Great Britain by David Fulton Publishers 2000

Note: The right of Peter Hook and Andy Vass to be identified as the authors of this work has been asserted by them in accordance with the Copyright, Designs and Patents Act 1988.

Copyright © Peter Hook and Andy Vass 2000

British Library Cataloguing in Publication Data

A catalogue record for this book is available from the British Library

ISBN 1–85346–691–3

Typeset by FiSH Books, London
Printed in Great Britain by Bell and Bain Ltd, Glasgow

CONTENTS

ACKNOWLEDGEMENTS

We wish to express our thanks to the following.

Our wives for sharing the knowledge and understanding derived from being emotionally inspirational teachers.

Our children for their experiences of being taught and their insights into what makes a difference in classrooms.

The many teachers we have worked with in schools and workshops. Their feedback has been encouraging and provided invaluable support.

All the students we have worked with for confirming that what we believe in and what is contained here makes a difference.

The ideas and information here are the result of a long teaching career and an eclectic mix of working with some outstanding teachers, learning from our own experiences and reading avidly. We are always keen to acknowledge the influences on our work but if any have been omitted, it is not deliberate on our part. If you recognise something that we haven't credited you with, please let us know and we will make amends in the next book.

HOW TO USE THIS BOOK

- Make the information here relevant to you. There is a wide margin for writing ideas, jotting key words or noting some personal responses to questions posed both within the text and in the activity sheets.

- At the end of each chapter there are 'Questions for professional development'. These may be used as part of your portfolio.

Start by getting the big picture

- Scan through the book, stopping wherever you get the urge to do so. Look at the contents page and the key point summaries. Do whatever it takes for you to get a feel for what the book can do for you.

- Begin to make connections between the ideas, strategies and skills contained in the book and aspects of your own experience. How will what is on offer here support you in your classroom? In what ways does it match or connect with what you know already? What ideas are unusual or different to how you behave in class?

Formulate your own goals

- What is it *specifically* you want to know from this book? What do you need to know to become even better at what you do?

- What kind of things would you like to be able to do as a classroom leader?

Give us feedback

We are genuinely keen to receive *any* feedback and will make every effort to include it in newsletters, subsequent editions or other books. Do let us have:

- further questions you may have

- experiences of implementing the strategies

- any successful ideas or variations you have discovered

- ideas that haven't worked (yet!).

Please contact us by E-mail:
PeterHook@phtcs.demon.co.uk

or

andy@munrotraining.freeserve.co.uk

Or by post:
Andy or Peter
c/o CEM,
Red Lion House,
9–10 High Street,
High Wycombe,
Bucks. HP11 2AZ

Introduction

THE JOURNEY CONTINUES

If you are doing something that doesn't work, the more you do it or the harder you try to do it the more it doesn't work.

Richard Bandler

Welcome to the second book to support what we hope remains a stimulating, enjoyable and rewarding career in teaching. An opportunity to make a real difference to your students. What greater challenge can anyone have than to make a positive difference, however small, to someone's life and what greater satisfaction comes from that knowledge?

You may think now of people who created that small (or major) therapeutic force in your life. Who were your favourite teachers, the ones who inspired you and made you feel important? The ones who you saw as having confidence in you, who made the time to listen and valued what you said. As you think of those people, what was it about them that can still create these emotions in you? Of course they had a style and manner of working with their students and obviously the things they said and the way they said them made a big difference.

What we're asking you to consider now is...

- **What beliefs did they hold that allowed them to be this way?**

- **What were the values that directed their behaviour?**

- **How were they able to create for themselves the physical state and intellectual frame of mind to persistently and unconditionally create that spark in you and many others?**

- **What part of them did they allow you access to?**

Our belief is that these people you have been thinking about had one thing in common. They believed with a passion that what they were doing was right. They had a vision of how they wanted the emotional, intellectual and physical climate of their classrooms to be. They articulated and lived those beliefs and visions – they 'walked the talk'. They also had realistic beliefs about what teachers do. They appreciated the personal qualities they possessed. They understood how these supported and encourage them in their classroom leadership. Most of all, they passionately cared about how to help their students become 'winners'.

Take responsibility

What, in the context of your classroom are you responsible for? Is responsibility the same as control? If there are things happening that you do not like in your classrooms and you do not take responsibility for managing them, you won't be able to change them. It is always easier to find reasons why we can't do something. Beware of giving mental space to problem-centred thinking that attributes causation and blame on parenting skills, the home environment, scarce resources, school management, the National Curriculum, government policy, OFSTED, etc. While we can't control how Nathan spends his time in the evenings, or the fact that he comes from a violent and dysfunctional family and arrives in school tired and very hungry, we can take responsibility for how *we* respond to this baggage and how we manage his behaviour. Pay attention to what you can do something about. That's what we mean by taking responsibility. If what you try doesn't work – do it differently. That's also what we mean by responsibility.

Take action

To bring about change you have to actually do something that is different. To move along your journey to the kind of classroom you want, to becoming the kind of teacher you wish to be, requires that you do something to make it happen. Often this will mean taking a risk, leaving your comfort zone and on many occasions getting it wrong. Students do not expect teachers to be perfect. They expect them to be human, to be fallible and to be able to deal with it honestly and with humility.

There are a number of skills that are common to highly effective teachers. In this book you will certainly gain an insight into those skills but more than that you will have access to the beliefs that effective teachers hold about themselves and their students. Not just what effective teachers do but also how they manage to do it.

Keep an open mind

If, as you use this book, you spend time noticing what we haven't included, you'll be right but you will also be wasting precious energy. If you think about the times when some of the skills wouldn't work, you'll be right again.

If, however, as you read this book we engage you in thinking about things you'd like to be able to do, we recommend you devote energy and time into learning how to do them.

Chapter 1

SETTING THE EMOTIONAL CONTEXT

Our evidence suggests that many children who behave badly in school are those whose self-esteem is threatened by failure. They see academic work as competitive and the competition as unwinnable. They soon realise that the best way to avoid failure in such a competition is not to enter it.

The Elton Report

In *Confident Classroom Leadership,* the emphasis was on the ways in which you can positively influence and effectively manage the behaviour of the students in your classes. Part of this process involved exploring how you could take responsibility for your own behaviour. For example, in how you respond to the choices students make and how you can be proactive in setting and maintaining an agenda which gives both choice and responsibility to the students.

In this book, we will revisit some of the key issues of choices and consequences and develop them further to offer deeper understanding and insights. We will also explore many additional perspectives that contribute to and support your journey towards a 'winning classroom'.

The quote above from Lord Elton's 1989 report into discipline in schools makes a clear and still relevant connection between academic study and emotional response in terms of self-esteem and describes by implication, those whose emotions are threatened by school, as losers. You will, we are sure, be familiar with students who still 'fit' Elton's description today.

In writing this book, we made a conscious decision not to focus on what could be described as the curriculum or academic component of classroom life. Clearly, we recognise the requirements and accompanying expectations, indeed pressures, of working within the national agenda of raising achievement. Indeed, we would argue that this book makes a valuable contribution in its own way to that agenda. However, we do not intend to add to the many excellent books that deal with learning styles and accelerated or brain based learning currently in print. We offer instead a list of resources and suggested reading. In particular, we would draw your attention to the work of Mike Hughes. His approach to learning, we believe, makes a valuable contribution towards creating a winning classroom. To illustrate this we have reproduced in Figure 1.1 some of his ideas on the nature of effective learning. However, there are two factors that have influenced our decision to adopt a different perspective – factors that we consider to be of greater significance in creating winning classrooms and that often appear to be overlooked in the debate about successful teaching and learning.

Firstly, there is the mindset that accompanies the word *'delivery'*. In recent years, much emphasis has been placed on 'delivering the curriculum'. The phrase is used with alarming regularity in connection not only with schemes of work and programmes of study, etc., but also to describe the process of what occurs in classrooms. Our experience of leading training workshops and working with schools on consultancy and support programmes is that many teachers, almost by default, believe that 'delivering' the curriculum is a key responsibility and expectation. We disagree! Our belief is that we *teach* the curriculum and this requires a different set of skills entirely.

As a householder, you will receive deliveries of mail. You may have newspapers and milk delivered too. Our guess is that these are quite incidental transactions in your lives and that, generally speaking, the relationships you have with these people are not significant or meaningful.

It is our view then, that the repeated emphasis on the need to 'deliver' the curriculum has tended to obscure the fundamental skills required to build relationships with students thereby creating the platform for a successful classroom climate. Certainly, as those of you who joined us on our Confident Classroom Leadership workshops testified, these skills are not part of Initial Teacher Training. To us, effective teaching and effective learning is about the micro skills of human transactions. The ways we build rapport, seeking to connect intellectually and emotionally with our students, recognising that their experiences and agendas are diverse and having the skill and desire to enter their world, are fundamental to the process of collaborating with them in creating successful and empowering educational experiences. As Mike Hughes (1999) states:

Learning is not done to people. It is done by them.

The second factor comes from the knowledge that exists about effective learning conditions. Recent developments in the understanding of neuroscience have allowed us to become more aware of brain functioning and in particular its significance in how learning occurs. There are many excellent books around now about brain based and accelerated learning and their effect in the classroom. All of them explore the impact of the emotional climate or 'learner state' as a vital component in effective learning. The emotional climate is directly conditioned by the quality of the relationships that exist in class.

The physical environment of the classroom will clearly impact on students' ability to learn as will, of course, the way the intellectual learning is structured. However, neither of these factors have as much influence as the emotional climate of your classroom. In situations where a student feels or perceives a degree of threat or negative stress, their ability to learn is greatly impaired. Dr Brian Boyd, writing in the *TES* (May 1997), suggested that we need to 'focus on the attitudes, motivation and self-esteem of young people'.

Put simply, what students think about their ability to learn, the climate in which they are asked to learn, the way they feel about themselves and their relationships with you and each other are too significant to be left to chance.

Our view may be simplistic but we challenge you to consider the context in which increasing numbers of students can be described as 'losers' in our educational setting. At no other time has greater concern been expressed about students who are variously described as 'demotivated', 'disaffected' or ' underachieving' in some way, while the Government's Social Inclusion agenda seeks to repair the widespread damage of missed educational opportunity.

A key theme in *Confident Classroom Leadership* was the degree to which you were able to acknowledge and accept responsibility for your own behaviour and recognise what aspects of classroom life were within your circle of influence. In creating a winning classroom, the basis of the question remains the same. In what ways can you proactively influence and teach the emotional curriculum in your class so that your students are able to feel that they can become winners?

In summary, we would like to remind you of one of Aesop's fables about the goose that laid golden eggs, an analogy we will expand on later in the book. We see academic success in its broadest sense to be the golden egg to which all those in education aspire. However, if the goose is not nurtured and maintained in a healthy and supportive way, eventually the goose will die and there will be no more golden eggs. If we want our students to not only learn intellectually but also develop healthy emotional intelligence, then we must proactively spend time maintaining the climate in which this can take place.

Key points

- Ignoring emotions inhibits the learning climate

- A wealth of information exists about learning

- We teach the curriculum

- Teaching is about interpersonal transactions

- Students need to be in the correct emotional state before learning can be effective

- The emotional climate of the classroom is significantly within your circle of influence

- Winning classrooms have proactive approaches to empowering emotional climates

Children learn effectively when they:

- want to

- are relaxed, yet alert

- are learning in their preferred style

- are actively engaged, i.e. doing something

- encounter something unusual, dramatic and unexpected

- regularly review what they have learned

Reproduced from *Closing the Learning Gap* with kind permission of Mike Hughes. Hughes, M. (1999) *Closing the Learning Gap*. Stafford: Network Educational Press.

Figure 1.1

Questions for professional development

What do you feel about the topics covered in this chapter?

What are some of the implications of the topics within your classroom?

What is it most important to you to remember from this chapter?

Chapter 2

CREATING AN EMOTIONALLY INTELLIGENT CLASSROOM

Your success as an educator is more dependent on positive, caring, trustworthy relationships than on any skill, idea, tip or tool.

Eric Jensen

As we said in the Introduction, this book is about the emotional climate of classrooms. In this chapter we consider the significance of emotions in successful teaching by offering a introduction to the notion of emotional intelligence and exploring two other key components we feel contribute to an emotionally empowering classroom.

In some form you are likely to spend a reasonable amount of time planning lessons, organising what you are going to teach, how you are going to teach it, what resources you require and so on. It is also likely your plan will include some idea or vision of what you want your students to achieve. In *Confident Classroom Leadership* we stressed the importance of including in your plans the concept of planning for good behaviour too. In other words, positive behaviour was too important a factor in successful teaching to be left to chance. This planning process is a natural way of creating action steps towards your goal or desired outcome for your students.

In this chapter we make the case for a further dimension to that planning – a consideration of emotional development. We do this not to add additional burden but for the simple reason that again, it is too important to be left to chance. The emotional climate of your classroom will either support or inhibit students in their journey towards academic and social growth and learning.

Classrooms are emotionally complex and dynamic organisations and as with all human activities involving human interaction, nobody can offer definite guidelines on how to cater for every situation. However, the insights and understandings we offer here and throughout the book, build carefully from *Confident Classroom Leadership* to provide you with developing awareness as to the significance and impact of your role in contributing to an emotionally empowering classroom.

Emotional intelligence

Peter Salovey, a Harvard psychologist, first used the phrase 'emotional intelligence' in 1989 to describe a range of skills and qualities he felt were significant factors in success. He included the following:

- a conscious understanding of feelings

- how to effectively manage those feelings in socially appropriate ways

- empathy

- responsibility and self-motivation

- an ability to resolve interpersonal issues.

He defined emotional intelligence as,

the ability to monitor one's own and others' feelings and emotions, to discriminate among them and to use this information to guide one's thinking and actions.

Daniel Goleman's best seller in 1996, *Emotional Intelligence*, which described a range of studies and research issues, was one of the first books to raise awareness widely about the significance of emotions. It made the point that emotions were not just intangible things that happened but chemical and neurological responses essential for both survival and well-being.

The significance and challenge for us as teachers is that Goleman cites studies which suggest that emotional intelligence or EQ is a more accurate predictor of success than academic intelligence or IQ. He states that,

At best IQ contributes about 20 per cent to the factors that determine life success.

As a classroom teacher you and the students interact on a daily basis. All of you have varying emotions surrounding those experiences and interactions we call lessons. In other words, emotions are unavoidable. To what extent do your emotions affect the way you interact with students? Imagine yourself walking slowly to your room with thoughts running through your head of how difficult this particular lesson or that particular child is going to be. What about the squabbles and arguments we get into with some children? How much do they contribute to the learning?

Learning, in all the forms in which it occurs in your classroom, takes place at a sensory level as well as an intellectual level. Decisions and choices, responses to internal and external stimuli such as language patterns, belief systems, assumptions and interpretations surrounding non-verbal cues will all involve feelings and emotions as well as what we conventionally describe as more rational or cerebral processing.

Indeed, Goleman emphasises the close connection between the role of emotions and academic success, stressing that the development of emotional intelligence increases our ability to learn effectively. He makes the point that emotional competence needs to be taught to children in schools and offers

> *abilities such as being able to motivate oneself and persist in the face of frustrations, to control impulse and delay gratification, to regulate one's moods and keep distress from swamping one's ability to think, to empathise and hope*

as a rationale.

Imagine, for a moment, that all the children in your class were highly skilled in the qualities associated with emotional intelligence?

What would that be like? How would it make a difference?

How would you feel about your work?

What would you be doing differently?

What impact would this have on the opportunities to learn?

A reasonable question would be at this point – 'OK, *so emotional intelligence is important but what do I do about it?'*

Our experiences of working on the emotional curriculum at KS 1 and 2 through circle time activities, through introducing children to the language and vocabulary of emotions and through modelling and verbalising our own emotional processes has proved to be valuable in reducing conflict and encouraging a calmer more productive working environment.

In KS 3 and 4, PSHE and the supporting activities undertaken by form tutors offer scope for developing programmes of study to explore emotional responses. It is also possible to introduce emotional concepts into a variety of subject areas. Some subjects lend themselves readily to developing skills of empathy while others encourage self-control, cooperation and problem solving.

(Further practical suggestions for developing the language of emotion are given in Chapter 7.)

However, we should never underestimate the power of modelling. Our students learn in many subtle and more overt ways through the interactions we have with them in class. Here are some examples of what we mean.

- Understanding and expressing emotional needs clearly
  'When you shout out, I feel frustrated because I can't help Nico as much as I would like to'

- Providing positive feedback
  'I like the choices you're making today Jack'

- Expressing empathy
  'I expect you are annoyed at staying back to talk about your behaviour and we need to find a solution to this together'

- Connecting positive actions to positive identity
  'Thanks for helping Liz today Shaquib. It showed me you understood her frustration'

- Sharing personal emotional responses
  'I was so embarrassed doing that assembly I just wanted to run away! I managed to remind myself to breathe deeply and remember other scary things I'd handled successfully'

A focus on success

'Nothing succeeds like success' is an old maxim. Winning classrooms have a focus on success because the ability to succeed is a powerful and empowering emotional state. Of course success comes in many guises and not merely in academic achievement. Successful interactions between teacher and student may be as simple as a welcome and greeting at the start of the lesson or appreciating some assistance in handing out work. Emotional success may be recognised by acknowledging good choices a student has made about their behaviour or work. It can be in your own behaviour as a teacher – the way you demonstrate your respect for them and your commitment to them being successful.

In what ways do you provide opportunities in a range of contexts for successful experiences? How do the students you teach feel when they think about coming to your classroom?

What opportunities do I offer for students to demonstrate success?

In how many different contexts is success recognised?

Are there any students in my classes who are excluded from success?

What similarities and differences exist between my ideas of success and those of my students?

How regularly do I give feedback on their success?

How do I celebrate success in my classroom?

Who else do I share our successes with?

A metaphor we like for thinking about success is that of an escalator moving upwards. As it's continually moving, entering the classroom becomes synonymous with stepping onto the escalator. At some level then, each student entering the class will move upwards, i.e. be successful however small that movement may be. It also allows for the possibility of that success to be in a range of contexts, emotional, social or academic. As with escalator travel, some people stay firmly wedged on the right, biding their time, whereas others will want to be racing up the left hand side in a rush to get somewhere. Some occasionally stand in the middle, getting in the way, but they too are trying to get somewhere!

> **You might like to think of a class now and imagine them on the escalator.**
>
> **Put faces to the people on each side.**
>
> **What kinds of things are they saying about the journey, verbally or non-verbally?**
>
> **Notice how they step onto the escalator. Are some of them hesitant, nervous, appearing worried about committing themselves to trying to be successful?**
>
> **Are there any that haven't stepped on yet?**
>
> **What's stopping them?**

Something that we find useful for increasing successful interactions in class is finding out what skills and resources students demonstrate away from class. We believe that resources are transferable from context to context. However, it often takes someone to point out the value of this process.

For example, we found it incredibly enlightening when on field trips to witness very competitive students forsake the chance to get to the top of a mountain walk first to drop to the back and support a struggling classmate. Equally, we have worked with very 'tough' and emotionally reticent Year 6 students who run a very different emotional programme becoming calming and sensitive to others' needs when reading to children in Reception.

Perhaps you know a child who is a primary carer for an invalid parent or spends a lot of time being responsible for younger siblings? Maybe you have in mind a student who would be the first to put an arm round a distressed friend or to walk a team-mate away when they have 'lost the plot'.

Returning to Salovey's indicators of emotional intelligence for a moment, the above examples are not only demonstrations of successful management of emotions, they are valuable resources to draw on in other contexts.

The student on the mountain was able to defer gratification (of getting to the top first). This ability can be useful in delaying going out in order to get coursework completed.

We recently worked with a student who was finding learning in science difficult and his behaviour had deteriorated in response to his own negative experiences. He was a member of a local theatre group and had absolutely no problem learning his lines, which he did by walking around at home and reading them out loud. He was very surprised when we suggested that he revised for science in the same way but it soon provided him with experiences of success and his behaviour improved in direct relationship to his emotional well-being!

As a teacher you will spend much of your time creating situations that you hope will give children successful experiences and make them feel positive. This will be true not just for the academic curriculum but for the social and emotional aspects of the classroom too. However, there will be times when students get frustrated because 'it's hard', they are stuck or feel they are not making progress or they run into relational difficulties. In these circumstances the model of the escalator can be useful too. By offering feedback using 'escalator language', i.e. language which retains an impression of moving forwards still, you can keep intact a positive emotional state for the student.

Escalator language contains lots of temporal words, which indicate that it's just a matter of time. It also retains a balanced perspective of the difficulty by keeping things in small chunks. Here are some examples

Which *bit* can't you do Jeff?

OK. It's *just* that bit you haven't done *yet*.

You don't feel you've done enough *so far?*

Sometimes it can be frustrating.

Another technique we find valuable in supporting successful outcomes for students is the use of exceptions. This works on the principle that there will always be a time when the difficulty or problem, be it academic or relational, either does not occur or is less intense. What happens at those times will give the student clues as to how they can move towards a solution.

> *'What happened last time you wanted to give up and didn't? How did you achieve that?'*

> *'Most of the time you can stay calm in class. How do you do that?'*

Building relationships

Dr William Glasser states that, '*Quality is always the product of warm, caring human relationships*'.

Building positive relationships between you and your students and encouraging them in the skills to relate well to each other is a key component of a winning classroom. Indeed, we believe that everything that happens in a classroom is by invitation as we cannot *make* students do things in a power struggle or purely coercive way. It becomes vital therefore, that as teachers, we take primary responsibility for being proactive in ensuring the relationships we achieve in class are as positive and empowering as possible.

Again, as with other aspects of a winning classroom, things do not happen by default. If we seek productive and positive relationships in class as a basis for supporting an emotional climate which empowers, we will need to invest time, energy and commitment towards achieving that goal.

We offer a four part model of building relationships here that emphasises the process by which the emotions involved in positive interactions can be encouraged. Additionally, it is skill based, with a focus on shared responsibility and choice which are key ingredients of empowerment.

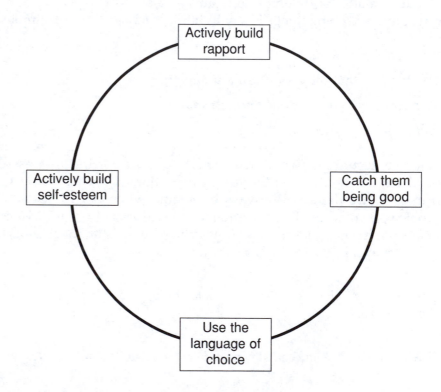

Figure 2.1 A model of relationship building

Actively build rapport

This is the process by which we make an essential connection with our students. Each transaction we have, both verbal and non-verbal, will add to or erode this sense of being comfortable together that we seek to create. Anthony Robbins (1988) refers to rapport as 'the relationship of responsiveness' and suggests, correctly in our view, that it is one of the most important skills to possess.

When you share rapport it makes much of what you do together easier, more productive and certainly more enjoyable. In fact it is a prerequisite for creating a winning emotional classroom.

Establishing rapport requires effort and commitment and a willingness to be responsive. It also requires a degree of sensory awareness since building rapport is done through noticing people's responses and modulating your actions. Of course you can only build rapport if you are genuine about having positive relationships and sincere in your desire to support students towards success.

There are many ways teachers establish rapport with students, many of which you will be doing already. Here are some examples.

- Social greetings using names at the start of lessons by way of a welcome and also away from class time such as playgrounds and corridors.

- Showing interest in their likes and dislikes away from school.

- Valuing their opinions without having to agree with them.

- Demonstrating trust and confidence in them.

- Accepting mistakes are normal occurrences.

- Subtly matching their physiology by smiling when they smile, respectfully mirroring facial expressions and gestures.

To create a winning classroom you will need to exert influence over your students to the extent that they feel that buying into your vision provides them with the answer to 'what's in it for me?' We have never managed to influence anyone when there has been an emotional distance between us. The bottom line is that in order to influence people, you need to enter their model of the world so that you can lead, guide and pace them on a journey that they will be willing to accompany you on.

Catch them being good

Although it may be stating the obvious, being acknowledged for a positive contribution is an emotionally uplifting experience. What we mean by catching them being good is being aware of the balance we achieve between noticing students getting it right and the amount of correction (or moaning) we do. We also mean that it is important to acknowledge, recognise and appreciate the things that the vast majority of students do on a regular basis – the kind of things that they are expected to do.

Like us, you may find the 'busy-ness' of today's classrooms makes it difficult to always remember to do this. It may even have led you to over-focus on students who get it wrong. Here are a few ideas to help to keep the focus on positive comments and acknowledgements.

- Use a little mantra that you repeat frequently – *'stop, scan, catch them being good'*.

- Place posters that have a positive image for you or affirmations on all four walls so that you have visual reminders.

- Involve the students. Tell them what you'll be looking for to praise during a particular session. They'll help to remind you!

If you have any special or unusual ways of keeping a positive focus then please send them to us. We'll acknowledge them and try to include them in *Teaching with Influence*.

Use the language of choice

If you accept the reality that as teachers we can't *make* people do things, then it follows logically that they are making choices about their behaviour and academic effort. Naturally, the more supportive, socially acceptable and academically progressive choices that students make the more we move to what we regard as a winning classroom.

In recognising and acknowledging the choices students make, even those that do not contribute positively to classroom success, we are providing opportunities for students to take responsibility for their actions.

In Chapter 4 we include a more detailed analysis of the relationship between choice and consequence and how that contributes to the emotional climate of the classroom. However, a point worth emphasising here is the empowering nature of being able to choose. The concept of self-determination and sense of control over what happens to you is a powerful and generally positive emotive experience. The opposite state would be to experience someone exerting unwanted power over you, feel coerced and maybe manipulated and that's an altogether different emotional experience.

Further, if you accept that you make a choice, should you make one that turns out to be a bad choice it is possible and therefore optimistic and hopeful to make a different one next time – again, a positive emotional experience.

We talk about using 'the language of choice' because language helps to connect students to the many choices they make on a daily basis. What we aim to do through language use is (a) let them know that we recognise they have made a choice and (b) offer feedback on the appropriateness of the choice. This is why in our classrooms you will hear us using, in age appropriate ways, phrases like,

'I'd like you to choose to get back to work now. Thanks.'

'How did you choose that answer?'

'I like the way you're choosing to work today Sam.'

'That's a really exciting choice of words Jenny.'

'Shaquib, if you continue to choose to talk, you'll be choosing to see me later.'

Actively build self-esteem

Self-esteem is a complex and dynamic collection of human emotions. Most teachers if you ask them can name students who have high or low self-esteem. However, often it's regarded as a fixed commodity and that is an unhelpful as well as an inaccurate view. Winning classrooms have a focus on proactively raising self-esteem. At a basic level, if people do not feel good about themselves physically and emotionally then success and achievement come that much harder. The issues and understandings in building a positive and proactive self-esteem classroom are detailed and complex. Because of this we have devoted the whole of Chapter 3 to the development of self-esteem within a winning classroom.

Key points

- Plan for the emotional curriculum as well as the intellectual and behavioural

- EQ predicts success more accurately than IQ

- All learning occurs at a sensory or emotional level

- Teach students the language and vocabulary of emotions

- Keep your classroom success orientated

- Be aware of people's resources in other contexts and encourage them to connect with them

- Use language patterns to keep students connected to moving forwards

- Work within a model that supports proactive approaches to building relationships

- Rapport is the key to influencing emotion

Activity 2.1 – Considering emotional literacy

For each of the areas of EQ below, list for yourself and for your students three opportunities that occur on a regular basis, either within your classroom or around the school, to emphasise, model and teach these qualities.

- A conscious understanding of feelings

For myself:

1. _____
2. _____
3. _____

For my students:

1. _____
2. _____
3. _____

- How to effectively manage those feelings in socially appropriate ways

For myself:

1. _____
2. _____
3. _____

For my students:

1. _____
2. _____
3. _____

- Empathy

For myself:

1. _____
2. _____
3. _____

Activity 2.1 – continued

For my students:

1. _____

2. _____

3. _____

- Responsibility and self-motivation

For myself:

1. _____

2. _____

3. _____

For my students:

1. _____

2. _____

3. _____

- An ability to resolve interpersonal issues

For myself:

1. _____

2. _____

3. _____

For my students:

1. _____

2. _____

3. _____

Questions for professional development

What do you feel about the topics covered in this chapter?

What are some of the implications of the topics within your classroom?

What is it most important to you to remember from this chapter?

Chapter 3

SELF-ESTEEM

I have a dream – that someday every child in every school and at every grade level will have a class entitled 'Self-Esteem and Effective Living Skills'. It will show up on their schedule every day somewhere between English and math.

Jack Canfield

Introduction

Our intention in this chapter is to give you some insights and understandings regarding an extremely complex phenomenon – self-esteem. We all know that healthy self-esteem is essential for physical and mental well-being and success. We readily accept that students who have poor or damaged self-esteem are less likely to be successful in schools. We know that our self-esteem is somehow connected with our ability to cope with change, resolve conflicts, form and maintain relationships, learn, etc. The problem is that the development and management of self-esteem is such a complex process that we often use the label without understanding the underlying processes.

What is self-esteem?

Before reading on, take a moment to reflect on the following exercise:

> **Think of a student whom you currently teach and that you feel has poor or damaged self-esteem.**
>
> **What *specifically* is it about their behaviour that causes you to believe this?**
>
> **What is it about their relationships with their peers and you that identifies them?**
>
> **When you interact with them, how do you feel?**

We believe that an understanding of the processes that go to developing what we call self-esteem is crucial if we are to create classrooms within which our students can genuinely begin to believe in their own ability to become winners.

The phenomenon of self-esteem results from the interaction of two models that we build of our world – our self-image and our ideal image. Neither of these models is fixed and we are all constantly engaged in processes that test, modify and restructure them.

Self-image

Our self-image represents our collected thoughts, impressions and beliefs about who we are. It is a vastly complex model and relates to all the roles we fulfil in our lives.

Among other things, we are constantly engaged in the process of gathering information about:

- our physical appearance – what we believe we really look like;

- our functional competency – what we believe we can or cannot do in all areas;

- our emotional competency – what we feel, or emotionally experience, in relation to particular aspects of our lives;

- our social competency – how we relate to individuals and groups in our lives.

The development of your students' self-image began long before they ever encountered your classroom and will continue to develop throughout the rest of their lives.

Your students' self-image with regard to their ability to function in your classroom is constantly being modified, updated and reinforced in response to the constant stream of feedback that you and others provide. Through the feedback, intentional and unintentional, that you provide in your classroom, you can have a significant effect upon the models your students build in relation to their potential achievement.

This feedback may vary from the overtly damaging (and totally unjustifiable) 'Why do you keep being so stupid!' through 'Wrong again! – See me' written at the bottom of a piece of work, to a subtle shake of the head and slightly downcast eyes given by a teacher when a pupil has answered a question incorrectly. Equally, the feedback may be 'Brilliant! Well done!' through 'Good to see you back in school again. How are you?', to a smile and thumbs up when they have answered a question correctly.

Whether it is negative or positive, all of these forms of feedback are constantly and inevitably contributing to the development of the complex picture that we call self-image.

Think again of the student whom you identified earlier as having poor or damaged self-esteem.

Take your mind back to the last time you were in the classroom together.

What feedback did you provide that might have reinforced their image of themselves?

What feedback did you provide that would, even in a very small way, have provided an opportunity for them to build a more positive, constructive self-image?

List three things, that you are not already doing, that you could do the next time you are together to give the student positive feedback about themselves.

1. _____

2. _____

3. _____

What students *believe* is true about them and the manner in which you organise your classroom's emotional and social agendas to enable all of your students to build and maintain positive self-images, is at the core of the genuinely winning classroom.

Ideal image

Your ideal image represents your collected experiences, personal interpretations of what others value and who you want to be. It is the collection of your goals, aspirations, expectations and dreams. Your ideal image is directly related to your self-image.

We are constantly assimilating information to help us determine what constitutes 'success', what others value, and what we wish to aspire to in terms of the roles we perceive ourselves fulfilling within our self-image. You are probably all too aware of the number of times in your professional life that you are exposed to models of 'successful' teaching. It sometimes seems that it is impossible to pick up a newspaper, turn on the radio or watch the television without being told what the teaching profession should be doing!

Equally, in their lives beyond school, young people are bombarded with models of 'success'. Television shows, magazines and advertising hoardings bombard them with models of 'successful' youth. Similarly, in schools, our students are very aware of what we hold to be a successful student. At the time of writing, it is hard to find a pupil in secondary schools that doesn't 'know' that in order to be regarded as successful they should achieve 5 A–C grades at GCSE. At the primary school level, you would be hard pushed to find a student who didn't know what levels they should aspire to in their Key Stage 2 SATs. Even in schools that we have worked with that profess to value all of their students equally, regardless of ability, it is common to find the '5 A–Cs = Success' equation being used by students of all levels of ability.

List five characteristics of what you regard as a successful student in your classroom.

1. _____

2. _____

3. _____

4. _____

5. _____

How many of your students, at this time, are achieving this?

How many of your students, with support, could aspire to these characteristics?

How many students are you not hopeful for?

What can you do to help this last group of students feel a greater chance of success?

Our models of success are infinitely more complex than simple output measures such as exam results. As teachers, we each daily communicate to students the sorts of behaviours that are valued within our lessons. The ways we do this may not be as overt as published 'league tables'. They may be as subtle as a smile when a student answers a question in a particular way or a nod of approval when a certain student walks into the room. All of them are indicators to all of our students of the sorts of behaviours that are valued within our classroom.

We also need to be aware that it is not only positive models that students will aspire to. If a student is told often enough that they are 'difficult', naughty, bad, etc., they will eventually come to believe this is true about themselves (self-image) and, in lieu of any other way of achieving success, they will set out to be the best bad person they can be!

Self-esteem

Self-esteem is the judgement you make about the gap between your self-image and your ideal image. It is a changing, dynamic thing. It is not fixed. It varies with circumstance and can change in a matter of seconds.

If you are in a situation in which you are fairly confident of the likelihood of success then you are likely to feel good about yourself – positive, healthy self-esteem. If the circumstances suddenly change in a way that makes it highly unlikely you will be successful, your emotional state will rapidly change to match your new circumstances.

Also, healthy self-esteem does not require that you achieve every goal, live every dream, and live up to every expectation that is set for you. You merely need to feel that, at any given time, you are moving positively towards the ideal images that are relevant or important to you at that time.

The key factors associated with healthy self-esteem are:

- a sense of movement towards attainable goals and aspirations;

- having access to regular, accurate, positive information to build or support self-image;

- the willingness to try new things and take risks (see below);

- the readiness to accept positive information about oneself and to incorporate it into one's self-image;

- an ideal image that contains not only dreams and long-term aspirations but also realistic, achievable goals and expectations;

- a sense of personal security and confidence;

- a sense that one is able to be proactive – make choices about one's behaviour;

- a realistic understanding of the consequences of the choices one makes;

- a sense of self worth.

Classroom implications

There are two key processes involved in the development of our self-esteem that have direct relevance in developing winning classrooms. They are self-discovery and feedback from significant others.

1. Self-discovery

Students need to be given access to opportunities to explore their own identities and in particular discover their self-image and its relationship to their ideal image.

Specifically, we need to give them continued opportunities to:

- engage in activities that challenge them;

- engage in problem-solving activities;

- regularly take part in situations in which it is safe and legitimate to make mistakes;

- take part in learning experiences where they are enabled to explore the limits of their ability;

- become actively involved in a wide range of supportive social transactions and relationships;

- collaborate with and be given responsibility for others.

For each of the above consider how often, in your classroom, your students are engaged in learning experiences which will also give them opportunities for self-discovery.

Consider those students who might have less than healthy self-esteem. What do you do to help them engage in and learn from opportunities for self-discovery?

What else could you do?

2. Feedback from significant others

Significant others (parents, key friends, key relations, siblings, you) provide a mirror that reflects back opportunities for your students to examine their self-image and ideal image.

Within the classroom situation, you should never underestimate your significance in the development and maintenance of your students' self-image and ideal image. Even with those students who seem to constantly reject you, if you buy into these feelings of rejection the student will take your actions as confirmation that you don't like them and that they were right to get you to reject them!

Neutrality is not an option! You cannot be neutral in terms of the contribution you make towards your students' development of their self-image and ideal image. Even a complete lack of emotional involvement will be interpreted as significant information. The choice is yours. You can either choose to become proactive in the development of your students' self-esteem or you can choose to leave it to chance and misinterpretation.

The power and vital importance of the subtle transactions that occur between adults and students in determining both our self-image and ideal self models will be dealt with as an ongoing theme throughout this book and is at the core of the chapter on emotional bank accounts.

List five ways in which you currently proactively set out to give positive, self-image enhancing, feedback to your students:

1._____

2._____

3._____

4._____

5._____

List five alternative, subtle, strategies that you could begin to use in the near future:

1._____

2._____

3._____

4._____

5._____

Damaged or unhealthy self-esteem

If students are constantly experiencing situations in which they feel that...

- they cannot achieve the expectations that they believe significant others have for them;

- they will never be able to achieve the goals that are part of their ideal image;

- the dreams and aspirations they have for themselves are rendered meaningless or unattainable;

- they are constantly being told they are a failure

...their behaviour will change to compensate for the significantly increased gap between their self-image and their ideal image.

Faced with these situations, students may start to demonstrate

- a drop in levels of motivation;

- feelings of self-doubt and reluctance to engage in new activities;

- withdrawal from social situations – particularly new or less secure situations;

- inappropriate risk taking.

They will tend to engage in one of the following two alternative strategies – as will all of us because this is part of normal human behaviour.

1. Opting out behaviours

Opting out behaviours are simply that. They are designed to remove you, physically or psychologically, from the situation. Teachers working in schools with a high percentage of students with 'difficult' behaviours frequently have significantly higher rates of teacher absenteeism which cannot be explained simply through illness. Many of us will walk away from potentially difficult situations as a coping mechanism.

Many teachers will agree that you can never get the parents whom you really want to see to attend parents' evenings. Opting out behaviour is one of the key reasons. In the same manner that it is difficult to avoid the unrealistic teaching models that are put forward in the media, so it is with parenting. It frequently seems that everybody from the Prime Minister, through the press and other media to the 'man in the street' is expounding a model of parenting that very few of us could ever live up to. These parents 'know' as part of their self-image that they are not that sort of parent. They do not perceive themselves as 'successful' parents. Consequently the easiest way to avoid the conflict between their perception of themselves as parents and what they believe are the school's models of 'success', is simply not to attend.

All of us are aware of the students who use this strategy as a means of avoiding failure. Many of them cause us to look despairingly at our attendance figures. Others simply skip individual lessons. Even more students quietly withdraw to the back of the classroom and refuse to put their heads over the 'barricades'. Whether it be passive or active opting out behaviour, the positive effects upon the students are the same – it temporarily reduces their feelings of potential failure.

2. Inappropriate compensatory behaviours

An alternative to opting out is to begin to take an action that makes you feel better about yourself. We start to display behaviours that we feel we can be successful at as a substitute for facing a situation of perceived failure. The consequences of these behaviours may seem to the outside observer to be counter-productive, but to the person utilising them they are stress reducing. These inappropriate compensatory behaviours (ICBs) can take many forms. They may be the 'bigger', more overtly difficult behaviours such as direct challenges to people in authority, or they may take more subtle forms. None of these ICBs are usually successful as long-term solutions to the individuals' perceived difficulties. Rather, in the short term, they serve to reduce the uncomfortable emotional and physical symptoms of stress.

Some students learn that they can gain a sense of personal success via their ability to 'wind up' or overtly challenge teachers. Therefore when faced with a situation which they predict may spell failure, their behaviour may become confrontational or aggressive. This tactic can occasionally also be seen to be used by parents faced with the prospect of coming into school – they will use their ability to become verbally aggressive and confrontational as an alternative to taking the risk that their parenting skills may be called into question. Many teachers find themselves at the 'rough end' of this overly aggressive style of avoidance behaviour! Equally, when a teacher's authority is overtly and publicly challenged by a student, some feel themselves to be under threat and respond in an aggressive, dominating style.

ICBs do not always take the form of big, overt behaviours. They may take the form of smaller, but to teachers equally difficult to manage, behaviours. One only has to observe a set of candidates immediately prior to an interview to see a fascinating display of low-level ICBs – fidgeting, fiddling, inappropriate eye contact, aimless wandering, stilted conversation, obsessional hair combing and clothes rearrangement, etc. Many of these behaviours are identical to those reported by teachers as high frequency but low-level disruptive classroom behaviours. Again, to the observer these behaviours may seem to serve no purpose but to the student they are extremely useful – 'I might fail if I try to answer these questions, but I will feel successful if I tidy my pencil case'.

Some students feel so threatened by their perceptions of failure associated with school that they build themselves a self-esteem protection shell. They put on a persona, which enables them to feel that they can cope. All too often this persona takes the form of 'streetwise' attitude and clothing. What they are really saying is that they feel vulnerable as themselves, but if they wear this tough outer shell they feel good. If we direct our attention towards trying to manage and teach the shell we will get nowhere. What we know about highly successful classroom leaders is that they seem to have the ability to see through the 'shell' and make contact with the vulnerable child inside.

This is perhaps one of the greatest skills involved in creating winning classrooms – the ability to see the child inside their shell and to create a classroom (and hopefully a school) in which children feel safe enough to leave their shells at the classroom door or school gate.

Self-esteem, skills and risk taking

Some people have suggested that it is possible to improve self-esteem by giving more skills. We would wish to qualify this. There is certainly a correlation between skill and self-esteem but they are not mutually dependent. An elegant but simple metaphor to describe why self-esteem is not a simple skills-based issue was taught to us by Jack Canfield (one of the great authors on the subject of self-esteem) and, with our own modifications, goes something like this:

> **Let us, for the sake of argument, say that we are able to pluck two teachers from their day-to-day jobs at White Knuckle Ride High School and offer them the opportunity of a lifetime. No longer will they have to face the daily trip into school. No more lesson preparation. No more marking. No more difficult students last thing on a Friday. Instead of all this, we are going to send them off to Las Vegas! Once there, they will attend the foremost poker school in the world. They will learn to play the game of poker at the feet of the Masters. Once they have both attained the peak of poker playing abilities, we will bring them back to England and set them up in one of the country's most prestigious poker games. The only difference between the two will be that we will give one of them £5,000 and the other £50. Which player do you think is most likely to take risks?**

Self-esteem is not wholly about the skills a student has. These undeniably help, but are not the whole picture. The most crucial factor is what they have in their emotional 'bank'. Students who find themselves in situations where they believe they are likely to be unsuccessful are less likely to take risks with either their learning or behaviour. They already feel negatively about themselves; they will not take the risk of further failure by trying something new. (The concept of the emotional bank account is so crucial it is both a chapter in its own right and a constant theme throughout the rest of this book.)

Changing our behaviour is risky. We know we have not tried to behave in the new way before so it is often difficult for us to predict if we will be successful. What do we do? We look back into past experiences of change. If our previous experiences of change have been of a lack of success and a feeling of failure then all the evidence will point towards this lack of success, and consequently uncomfortable emotional responses, being repeated. We will have very few funds in our emotional 'bank'. The likelihood is that we will resist the change even before we attempt it.

Students who have a poor self-image and find it difficult to believe that they can live up to many of the in-school success models they believe are being set for them also find it difficult to take the risk of changing their behaviour. For them it is better to continue to be, in our terms, 'unsuccessful' at their present level than to take the risk of even greater 'failure' by behaving in a different way.

Think about a typical lesson that you have taught recently.

In what ways did you make it emotionally safe for your students to try out new academic and social behaviours?

Which of your students do you think find it difficult to face the risk of changing their behaviour?

In what additional ways might you support these students?

Self-talk

Do you talk to yourself about you? Of course you do. You probably just did!

All of us are engaged in a constant conscious and unconscious dialogue with ourselves. The nature and quality of this internal dialogue is largely determined by our internal assessment of ourselves and our beliefs about the world we live in – our private assessments about the relationship between our self-image and our ideal image. Students who habitually talk in a positive way to themselves will be those we describe as 'upbeat', 'lively', 'interested', 'happy', etc. Students who talk to themselves in a habitually negative way will tend to appear as 'uninterested', 'morose', 'sullen', etc.

In our workshops we use a simple little demonstration to illustrate the power of this internal dialogue in determining how we feel about ourselves. It is called the 'Green Hair Game' and goes something like this:

Us:	John, if I said that you had green hair, would that hurt you?
John:	No.
Us:	Why not?
John:	Because I know I don't have green hair.

It's not what we say to John that affects how he feels. What John believes about his hair before we say what we say is what determines his emotional response. If, for instance, John genuinely had green hair and was proud of it he would be pleased that we had noticed. On the other hand, if he had tried to dye his greying hair and it had gone wrong, he may well be distressed that we had brought it to everybody's attention.

If somebody calls you stupid and you feel hurt by it, they didn't hurt your feelings. It is your own self-doubt about your own ability that causes you to feel hurt. In order to feel hurt by being called 'stupid', many things have to be true for you. Some of the most significant are:

- You have to believe that you value the opinion of the person who is calling you stupid.

- You might have to have existing self-doubts about your abilities in the area in question.

- You have to believe that a lack of skill in this area is significant.

Students who have a wide range of negative beliefs and doubts about their abilities (academic and social) will consistently use negative internal dialogue about themselves and the events in their lives. They will be 'hyper-sensitive' to information that confirms their existing negative self-image and be rejecting of information that contradicts it. They are only emotionally 'comfortable' when being given negative information about themselves! It is for this reason that some students are extremely rejecting of any form of praise – it contradicts their negative view of themselves and they therefore only feel comfortable when it has been dismissed. In its more extreme forms, this behaviour gives rise to students who destroy any piece of work that teachers comment favourably upon!

It can be very revealing to try the following exercise.

Think of two students one of whom you would regard as having high self-esteem and the other low self-esteem.

(If you are teaching in K1 or K2 then you can do this exercise in one or two school days. If you are teaching in K3/4 then you will have to carry it out over four or five lessons.)

Listen carefully to the language that these students use in your classroom to interact with both their peers and yourself. In particular listen to the way they describe themselves, their work, their mistakes and their relationships. (The language we use is often a direct reflection of our internal dialogue.)

What did this tell you about the internal dialogue that these two students use to describe their worlds?

What proactive strategies could you use to ensure that your students begin to use more positive internal dialogue?

One particular piece of internal dialogue that many teachers fall foul of is the belief that 'Good teachers control the behaviour of all the pupils all the time'. This is a referential model that has destroyed many competent classroom practitioners and it is *totally and utterly wrong*!

- You cannot control the behaviour of your pupils – you can manage their behaviour.

- You cannot manage the behaviour of every pupil you meet – there are, unfortunately, some very damaged students in our school system.

- You cannot do it all the time – even the best of us have an 'off' day!

A more realistic and healthy piece of self-talk you can adopt for yourself is:

'Good teachers manage the behaviour of most of the students most of the time.'

This is realistic. It is achievable. It will not destroy you. Use it every day.

Key points

- Self-esteem is not a fixed quantity. It is the result of the dynamic relationship between your self-image and your ideal image.

- Within your classroom and in all of your other transactions with your students you are a significant factor in determining the development of your students' self-image and ideal image.

- Healthy self-esteem is at the core of achievement in all areas of our lives.

- Neutrality is not an option! Your choice is to either become proactive in managing your students' self-esteem or leave it to chance and hope for the best.

- We need to pay careful attention to the messages that we give to students about what is valued in our schools and classrooms.

- Students who develop damaged self-esteem will tend to resort to either opting out or compensatory behaviours.

- Self-esteem and skills are correlated but not necessarily mutually dependent.

- Students with damaged self-esteem will find it very difficult to change their behaviour – change represents risk.

- The student's internal dialogue (self-talk) plays a key role in determining how they interpret their world to themselves. Students who have negative self-talk in a large number of areas will place themselves into a spiral of decline.

- We need to be aware that learning, both social and academic, will only take place in environments within which, when students make mistakes with their behaviour, they will have their behaviour corrected in a way that protects their self-esteem.

Activity 3.1

Considering your classroom environment

The way we first encounter a situation can have a significant effect upon our whole experience of that situation. Therefore, this exercise invites you to explore the starts of your lessons from your students' point of view.

First impressions:

In your mind's eye, imagine being a student entering your classroom. As you enter the room what can you see that makes you feel welcomed and valued? Is there anything about the room that makes you feel good to be in there?

(Even if you teach in a wide variety of rooms over which you have little environmental control, this is a useful exercise as it will give you clues as to how much you need to compensate in other ways.)

Still from the point of view of a student, what little things, if they were changed, would make the room more welcoming to you?

List four things that you could change to make the environment more welcoming:

1. _____
2. _____
3. _____
4. _____

Initial transactions:

Now imagine that you are watching the start of one of your lessons. Imagine that you can take yourself out of your body and watch yourself and your students from one of the top corners of the room.

Watch and listen to the sorts of transactions that occur between yourself and your students as they arrive to your lesson.

What about these transactions might make students feel valued and welcome.

What about latecomers?

What about students who you find more difficult to manage?

List four things that you could change to make the initial transactions you have with students even more welcoming:

1. _____
2. _____
3. _____
4. _____

Questions for professional development

What do you feel about the topics covered in this chapter?

What are some of the implications of the topics within your classroom?

What is it most important to you to remember from this chapter?

Chapter 4

DEVELOPING PROACTIVITY AND RESPONSE-ABILITY

In proactive behaviour we take actions to create a future we want, or avoid a future we don't want.

Jack Canfield

Introduction

In *Confident Classroom Leadership* we looked at the 4Rs framework for establishing effective classroom agendas and we emphasised the point that the fundamental agendas that you establish and maintain within your classroom determine your success in implementing your day-to-day classroom leadership plan. They set the daily climate for the academic and social growth of your students. The basis of this agenda setting is your 4Rs framework of Rights, Responsibilities, Rules and Routines.

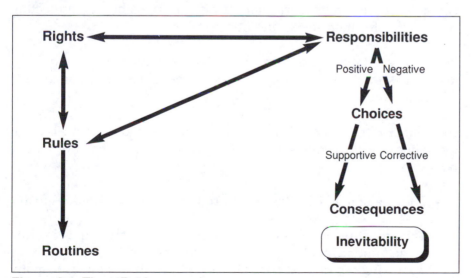

Figure 3.1 The '4Rs' framework

Firstly, we will deal briefly with the relationships between the 4Rs of rights, responsibilities, rules and routines and then move on to examine in greater detail the powerful links between responsibility, choice and consequence.

Rights, Responsibilities, Rules and Routines

Essentially, your decisions regarding the acceptability of the choices students make about their behaviour need to be firmly based upon your judgement about the extent to which a student's behaviour supports or infringes one of four basic rights. These are:

- Your students' right to learn

- Your right to teach

- Everybody's right to safety (physical and psychological)

- Everybody's right to dignity and respect.

These four basic rights enable you to go beyond the 'Because I said so!' approach. They enable you to easily deal with the student who instinctively responds to your corrective interventions with 'Why not?' or 'Why shouldn't I . . . ?'.

Rights and responsibilities are inseparable. One of our key behaviour management objectives must be to proactively teach the link between rights and responsibilities. If our students are to genuinely enjoy their rights then they must learn that they are responsible for protecting these rights for themselves and others.

Your rules establish the framework within which this is possible. Your rules must enable you to work effectively within your rights and responsibilities framework.

In *Confident Classroom Leadership* we suggested some essential guidelines for the establishment of classroom rules. They are set out below:

- They must refer directly to your rights and responsibilities focus.

- They must be few in number. No more than three rules for Key Stage 1 and then add one more rule for each additional Key Stage up to a maximum of six rules in Key Stage 4. If you have too many rules you, and your students, will forget to follow them.

- They must be phrased in a way that ensures your students are clear what you mean. 'Treat everybody nicely' is nowhere near as explicit as 'No swearing, name-calling or put-downs'.

- They must deal with behaviours that you can observe within your classroom. Don't have a rule about homework for example. Save this for one of your routines. You must be able to 'catch' your students following your rules.

- They need to be understood by your students and actively taught to them.

You must make a distinction between rules and routines. Routines refer to the administrative aspects and procedures necessary to help any complex organisation resist the slide into chaos. Clear routines are essential to the smooth running of your classroom. Your routines represent the specific set of behaviours that are at the core of helping your students become successful. The more precise you can be about your routines the more likely it is that your students will follow them.

The essential link between choices and responsibility

In *Confident Classroom Leadership* we emphasised the role that the language of choice plays in maintaining a calm emotional climate. In this section we will expand on the concept of choice and look at the essential role it plays in developing truly responsible, proactive students.

Look closely at the word responsibility. We would say that it is more usefully framed as 'response-ability' – literally the ability to choose your response to the circumstances you find yourself in. This is the true essence of empowerment. Knowing that you have a choice about the emotional response you use in a situation is the foundation stone of proactivity.

Many students – and many adults for that matter – do not believe that they manage their emotional lives. They believe other people or external events make them feel things. They will articulate this to you in the classroom. How many times have you heard a student say things like 'She made me hit her', 'He made me angry' or 'This work does my head in!'. How many colleagues have you heard say things like 'Shaquib makes me so annoyed when he does that' or 'Class 5 make me so cross'.

If I blame Shaquib for making me annoyed – I am not being proactive, I am being reactive. I am saying that Shaquib is determining my emotional state. Psychologically, I am empowering him to determine my emotional well-being. By making the choice to respond in this way I am disempowering myself. Overcoming the notion that external events and forces determine our emotional responses is at the heart of the empowering classroom.

Equally, by allowing students to continually blame others for their emotional responses – 'She makes me angry' – we are creating the classroom climate of disempowerment, of external determinism, for them. I am covertly teaching my students that they are not response-able. I am legitimising reactive rather than proactive behaviour.

Reactive teachers are frequently affected by the mood of their students. If the students come into the room bubbly and enthusiastic they feel good and the lesson goes well. If the students come in morose and reluctant they feel depressed and the lesson goes badly. The situation then becomes self-fulfilling because the students then begin to respond to the emotional state of their teacher. At the end of the lesson the teachers blame the students for the lesson outcomes and further confirm to themselves their disempowered state by saying things like 'I couldn't do a thing with them in the mood they were in today' or 'It was a really good lesson today, they were all in such a good mood'.

Proactive teachers treat the same situation in a very different way. They do not allow their students to choose their emotional state for them. They are proactive in determining their own emotional state. They are still affected by external stimuli – physical, social or psychological. The difference lies in that their choice of response to these stimuli is determined by their values and beliefs. They will be alert to the emotional climate that their students bring into the room but they will choose not to react to it. Rather they will use their value-driven approach to enable them to choose an emotional response that allows them to continue being effective.

Proactive teachers will be sensitive to the morose and reluctant attitude that students may be bringing into their lesson from outside and they will choose to adjust their response to begin to proactively re-establish a working relationship. Also they will be sensitive to the bubbly and enthusiastic mood of their students and choose to build on this to help them build even more secure relationships for the future.

So it is with our students. Both by example and by proactively teaching we need to bring our students gradually to the point where they too can become genuinely response-able. We can do this at a whole variety of levels.

At its simplest, we can change the language we use in our day-to-day communications within classrooms. Rather than saying 'Put your pencils down and look at me' we can imply a choice by saying 'Can you all choose to put your pencils down and look at me' – we will deal with what happens if they choose not to in a moment!

When dealing with the inappropriate choices that our students sometimes make, rather than saying 'Why did you hit Mary?' we can ask 'Why did you choose to hit Mary?'. Equally, when giving praise we can build in the notion of response-ability by using phrases such as 'I like the way you've chosen to set that work out John' or 'Thank you for choosing to sit down and wait patiently Javad'.

At an institutional level, we can proactively discuss the notion of choice in circle time, tutor time or PSHE activities. We can build the links between choice and responsibility into our assemblies. It can become part of the living framework of our classrooms and our schools. Where we have worked with schools to make this a reality the change in student attitudes towards relationships and learning have been remarkable.

It starts with you – developing personal proactivity

How proactive are you in your classroom? How often do you choose to allow yourself to blame external events and circumstances for your emotional responses? How often do you encourage your students to recognise that they have choices in their behaviour?

If you are feeling particularly brave, you might like to try the following exercise.

If you haven't already got one, beg or borrow a small tape recorder.

Set it up in a place close to where you do most of your teaching and tape yourself during a normal teaching situation.

When you are feeling fairly confident, review the language you use to communicate with your students.

Ask yourself two simple questions:

How frequently do you model proactivity and response-ability?

How often do you praise the positive choices that your students make?

Proactive teachers are very aware of what is and what is not within their ability to influence. They focus upon those areas of their lives over which they have direct influence. They are aware that there are many things over which they do not have any direct influence but they do not choose to spend their energies in these areas.

Reactive teachers are equally aware of both of these areas, but their response is very different. Typically, they expend their energies on those aspects of their lives over which they have little or no influence. Equally typically, these energies manifest themselves in blaming or frustration. They blame the parents, Government, society, the gene pool, anything! Certainly, these all have, to varying degrees, an effect upon the classroom learning and emotional climate but they are not normally under the direct influence of the teacher. The difficulty that many of these teachers are faced with is that the more they expend negative energy on the things over which they have little influence the smaller becomes the number of things over which they do have influence.

Teachers who focus their emotional energy upon choosing to become proactive about those things over which they have some direct influence become naturally more empowered. They begin to see real and lasting change. This, in itself, gives them more emotional energy, which leads to a greater expansion in the range of things over which they have influence.

You might choose to break from reading at this point and try Activity 4.1 at the end of this chapter.

Free or consequential choice?

Simply reminding Joe that he has a choice about his behaviour will not guarantee that he will choose appropriate behaviour. Joe is free to choose his actions but he is not free to choose the consequences of his actions.

We can decide to put our hand into a pot of boiling water but we cannot choose what will happen once it is in there. Joe can choose to swear at Michael but he cannot choose the consequences of that action.

From the choices we make in our lives flow the consequences. Sometimes, because we are not prepared to accept what we know will be the consequences of our actions, we choose to take a reactive, disempowered stance. Joe may think that the consequences of his choice – hitting Mary – will lead to a consequence that he wishes to avoid – staying behind after the lesson. Therefore Joe seeks to transfer the responsibility for his actions onto Mary – 'She made me hit her!'.

In every aspect of life, the choices we make cannot be divorced from the consequences that follow. So it must be in our classrooms. This is the 'night follows day' principle of management that we must ensure is consistently applied within our classrooms.

Our students must not only learn that they are response-able by being empowered to make choices, they must also learn that the choices they make come with predictable consequences attached. In *Confident Classroom Leadership* we made much of the need for consistency in the application of consequences and we do not intend to over-dwell on it here. Nevertheless, it is worth repeating the basic principle that learning is easiest if the outcomes of your chosen actions are known and consistent.

Making and correcting mistakes

There are times in our lives – as there are in our students' lives – when we make choices and subsequently become aware that we are not happy with the consequences of that choice. This is called a mistake. Mistakes are a natural part of the learning process. It is normal for our students to make mistakes. If we are going to create winning classrooms then the way we handle these mistakes is crucial.

If, when students make mistakes with their behaviour we treat them harshly then we are creating a problem for both our students and ourselves. Even worse, if we link our comments or actions following their mistake to implications that they are 'bad' people then we are committing one of the cardinal classroom sins.

The consequences that follow a student's choice should be as a natural result of that choice and preferably focused upon teaching alternative choices (see below). They should not be designed (either deliberately or accidentally) to wound, hurt, humiliate, demean or otherwise put down the student. Always, this sort behaviour from a teacher is simply the teacher demonstrating his or her own level of disempowerment. They have decided that the student's actions are causing them to experience undesirable emotional feelings – hurt, revenge, humiliation, etc. – and are adopting a reactive rather than proactive response.

If the consequences that follow a student's mistake are seen as too threatening by the student they will begin to develop strategies to avoid those consequences. They will blame, lie, avoid, distract, etc. In itself, this compounds the problem in that it is actively teaching the student the very behaviour we are trying to overcome – reactive disempowerment. We will be denying our students access to one of life's great educational experiences – learning from our mistakes.

Putting students into a position where they feel it is necessary to deny or cover up their mistakes further disempowers them in that, by not enabling them to admit them and accept the natural consequence, it inhibits them from moving on and learning. They will now be primarily focused upon maintaining the denial or cover up and the more forceful we become or the more severe we make the consequences, the more determined will be their efforts.

Teaching our students that it is normal to make mistakes and natural to be prepared to accept and, more importantly, learn from the logical outcomes of those mistakes is an essential and vital element of a winning classroom.

Working to solutions – consequences that go beyond sanctions

Many of us have had the experience of discussing consequences with students. In particular, you may have invited class members to suggest consequences that could be applied for students who have made a particular choice. Recently we watched a circle time session in a primary school when the topic for discussion was a fight between Erica and Peter that had occurred in class the previous day when the teacher was out of school. At first, the students were asked to suggest what should be the consequences of Erica and Peter's choices. Their list of possible consequences was:

1. Miss breaktime today.

2. After school detention.

3. Do extra work during lunchtime.

4. Make them sit apart for the rest of the day.

The teacher then asked the group another question – What possible solutions could there be that would help Erica and Peter to make better choices next time? Their list was very different:

1. Work together more often so that they start to make friends.

2. Ask a friend to help them when they start to feel angry.

3. Erica could tell Peter when she didn't like what he was saying and then walk away.

4. Peter could apologise to Erica and 'pay back' by helping Erica with her work.

The difference between these two lists gives us powerful information about the most effective way of interpreting consequences in our classrooms. The students' first list is simply a list of punishments disguised as consequences. Erica and Peter should 'pay' for their choices. At least 1 and 4 fit within the other 4Rs framework that tells us that consequences should be Related, Respectful, Reasonable and Revealed in advance.

The second list is very different because it moves away from the notion of 'paying for your mistakes' and focuses upon solutions that would help Erica and Peter to make more appropriate choices in the future.

Where do students learn to disguise consequences as punishments? Could it be from us? Almost always, in our discussions about consequences with teachers, they suggest that they would opt for consequences similar to those in the students' first list. They tend towards consequences that focus on the student having to pay for their mistake rather than looking for a solution that will help the student to make alternative choices next time.

The reason that the circle time conversation took place was that we were starting to work with the teacher in introducing to her students the notion of working towards solutions rather than sanctions. Whenever we have done this in the past in both primary and secondary schools, teachers report that it is a very difficult skill to learn but the benefits are enormous. The level of mutual respect and caring between the students rises dramatically. Students do not try to deny or distract from the natural mistakes they make. Both students and teachers can become even more proactive in their responses and therefore move even closer towards genuine response-ability.

This is not to say that we never use more traditional – Related, Respectful, Reasonable and Revealed in advance – consequences. When they are properly understood by students and utilised appropriately they become a natural part of the classroom's consequential environment. Rather, we find that they are rarely used. Traditional consequences have become only one, less favoured, option to support students. Teachers and students alike find consequences that are focused towards solutions are simpler, more easily delivered and accepted, fairer and, most importantly, more effective.

Key points

- The 4Rs framework of Rights, Responsibilities, Rules and Routines represents the fundamental agendas necessary for your day-to-day success in the classroom.

- One of our most important objectives for our students' personal growth must be to encourage the development of true responsibility – literally, response-ability.

- Before you can develop it in your students you must take personal response-ability for your own emotions.

- You must develop a proactive response to the events in your classroom – you must not let events dominate and dictate your emotional responses.

- The language of choice is essential in developing responsibility.

- You will waste vital emotional energy if you largely focus upon issues and events that are outside your direct influence.

- Choice is not free – choices bring with them consequences. The more predictable these consequences are, the more likely it is that students will learn to make consistent choices.

- Mistakes are natural. We need to ensure that the consequences that follow a mistake are not such that they cause the student to learn to deny or blame others for their choices.

- We need to ensure that, wherever possible, our consequences support and teach future choices not simply punish the past.

Activity 4.1

This activity is designed to help you start to clarify those aspects of your professional life over which you have direct influence and can consequently become proactive about. The exercise can be done individually, with a friend or colleague or in a group.

You will need a large sheet of paper divided into three columns and a supply of small cards or 'PostIt'-type notes.

Stage 1: List – one to each card or 'PostIt' – all the factors which cause you concern regarding both the learning and emotional climate of your classroom. These may vary from the simple such as 'Mary constantly calls out' through to the more complex such as 'Government policy on time allocation for Foundation Subjects'.

Stage 2: Head the three columns on your sheet of paper 'Not within my field of direct influence', 'Could become within my field of influence with the support/collaboration of others' and 'Normally within my field of influence'.

Stage 3: Sort your factors into the three broad categories. Take your time over this. Focus upon what you know is realistically achievable rather than your current reality. For instance, you may not have yet found a way of encouraging Mary to choose not to shout out but you probably know that if you focused upon it, it would be achievable.

Stage 4: Review your lists. Which do you currently spend most time focusing your emotional energies upon?

Stage 5: This is the hardest bit but will have the greatest benefits. Decide that over the next four weeks you will make every effort to focus your energies on two aspects only. Firstly, and the majority of your energy should be concentrated here initially, work on becoming proactive about the factors that are normally within your field of influence. Secondly, spend a lesser amount of emotional energy nurturing the collaborative relationships necessary to become proactive about the factors in your middle column.

Stage 6: Look at the list of factors in your 'Not within my field of direct influence' and take a proactive stance – smile gently at them. Accept them for what they are – part of the reality of life. Maybe as your ability to influence more and more of your classroom environment develops some of them may come into your field of influence. Some may never be there. That is the reality of life. Determine that, although they may be very real, you will no longer spend large amounts of emotional energy on them.

Activity 4.2

Developing supportive consequences

Think of a student for whom you are currently choosing to use more traditional consequences. List below the sorts of behaviours you are applying consequences to:

_____

_____

_____

What behaviours would you rather the student chose?

_____

_____

_____

What support could you choose to give the student in order to help them learn to make better choices in the future?

_____

_____

_____

Questions for professional development

What do you feel about the topics covered in this chapter?

What are some of the implications of the topics within your classroom?

What is it most important to you to remember from this chapter?

Chapter 5

NURTURING YOUR CLASSROOM'S EMOTIONAL BANK ACCOUNT

Your relationship with your students can take months to build and only seconds to destroy, so protect your investment and your integrity by being real and telling the truth.

Eric Jensen

Introduction

In the closing part of Chapter 1 we briefly mentioned Aesop's fable of the Goose that Laid the Golden Egg and suggested that the 'golden eggs' of the classroom are the levels of academic achievement, the targets achieved, the benchmarks attained. If that is the case, what is the Goose? We would suggest that your 'goose' is represented by the emotional state of your students. If you can maintain the correct emotional state, your students will continue to lay the golden eggs of achievement. If you neglect their emotional state, for a while the eggs will continue to come forth but gradually, little by little, the eggs will become less frequent. Eventually, if the neglect continues the goose will become terminally ill and egg production will cease altogether.

In his seminal book *The Seven Habits of Highly Effective People* (which, if you haven't already read, we would strongly commend to you for your own personal development), Stephen Covey makes much of Aesop's fable and develops it into what he calls the P/PC balance. P stands for production – egg laying – and PC for production capability – the health of the goose. In order to maintain a suitable supply of golden eggs we need to focus upon the long-term health and survival of the goose.

You will remember that in Aesop's fable the farmer decides to get all of the eggs in one go and kills the goose. When he reaches inside he finds the goose contains no more eggs. So it is in life. Short-term approaches, which attempt to produce lots of eggs in one go, are rarely successful. What ensures a steady supply of eggs over time is a focus upon maintaining the health of the goose.

Covey goes on to illustrate the importance of maintaining the P/PC balance in every aspect of our lives. In the next few pages, we would like to demonstrate how this simple notion can be translated into your classroom in a way that will dramatically enhance both the learning and social agendas.

Focusing upon relationships rather than results

Because of our situational position with regard to our students it is very easy to neglect the essential elements of the balance. Particularly when we ourselves feel under pressure to get our students to lay more and more golden eggs, it is easy to resort to attempting to squeeze the goose harder and harder. After all, we have authority, we are bigger, we are smarter, and we have status and can make things happen. We can tell them what to do and if they don't do it then we can make their life difficult. We can insist that they lay more golden eggs and if they don't we can make it very clear that they will not enjoy the alternative.

For some of our students, the less emotionally vulnerable, this will sometimes have the desired short-term effect. For the more emotionally vulnerable, it will create a terminal illness almost immediately. They will opt out, truant, refuse, work-avoid, and become openly defiant. Eventually, if we maintain the pressure, even the previously emotionally healthy students' ability to continually produce results will decline.

What about the alternative? What if we try to encourage them to lay more golden eggs through popularity? What if we give them their way, take off all pressure for results? In the short term this may produce more relaxed, happier students. They may start to produce a few more golden eggs simply because they like us. This will only work while they are unaware that we are only being nice to them to get them to lay more eggs. As soon as our ploy is discovered egg production will drop off or cease totally. Even if egg production continues it will be at an unjustifiable long-term cost to our students' production capability. We are not helping them learn to set and achieve targets. We are not helping them learn that they can become more than they are at present. We are not teaching them about self-discipline and personal responsibility. The most essential skills for becoming a successful adult are being omitted at the expense of obtaining more and more golden eggs.

Whether we choose to be overly-authoritarian or overly-friendly in our attempts to increase egg production, we will have made the serious mistake of focusing entirely upon the number of eggs obtained and not upon the health of the goose. What about our relationships with our students? What emotional strengths will we be developing to help them through the difficult times in their lives? What relationships will we have developed to enable us to support them during the tough times? What sense of self-discipline, personal responsibility, notion of choice, self-confidence and ability to achieve goals are we teaching our students?

In the winning classroom (and school) we need to be constantly focusing upon developing and maintaining the classroom relationships that make the production of results possible. We need to be constantly alert to resisting the pressures that can lead us to focus on getting the benefits, the golden eggs of improved academic achievement, at the expense of the health of the goose.

Understanding the classroom emotional bank account

We would like you to think of the emotional climate of your classroom as a bank account with you as the key depositor. Just like a conventional bank account, the more you deposit the more you can withdraw and when you go overdrawn there are penalties. Unlike your more conventional bank account, this very special account comprises a whole set of individual deposit boxes. Each one of these deposit boxes represents one of your students.

The only difference is that in this very special bank account your deposits can only be made in terms of your personal, proactive interactions with your students. The deposits will come in the form of the respect and courtesy you show, the kindness you display, the level of commitment you show towards their personal and academic success, the honesty you display in your relationships and the clarity of your positive expectations. The more frequently you make deposits into the account the greater the reserves you will accumulate to see you through the difficult times. These reserves are what we more normally call trust. They represent the extent to which your students have trust in you.

Unfortunately, at an individual student level, some of these deposit boxes come to you already in deficit. These are the students with whom you have to make that extra special effort to make sufficient deposits to bring them up to the same starting point as the rest of your students.

The more reserves you build up, the greater every one of your students will trust you and the more likely they are to continue to produce more and more golden eggs. If you have a large number of reserves in a student's individual deposit box you can even make mistakes in your relationships with them and that trust level will compensate.

If you develop the habits of showing discourtesy to students, giving no respect, showing no sympathy for their social or academic circumstances, showing no commitment to their success other than your need for greater golden egg production, then your reserves will soon dwindle. The trust level will be extremely low or non-existent. You will have no flexibility to make mistakes in your relationships. At the first possible occasion the goose will cease egg production all together. You will have to be extremely careful about everything you say or do. You will be walking on emotional eggshells. Beware! For students who come to you with very little already in their deposit box this process can be extremely rapid.

There is another peculiarity that you need to be aware of with this particular bank account – the deposits are extremely fragile and dwindle with time. The constant interpersonal transactions that occur in every classroom slowly, but inevitably, etch away at them. Particularly with older, more naturally emotionally volatile students, or with students who are coming from less emotionally nurturing environments, there may even be sudden withdrawals that you are not even directly aware of. It is not sufficient to make an extremely large deposit at the beginning of your relationship with your class and expect to be able to draw on it weeks or even days later. The deposits need constant replenishment.

If your account goes into deficit with a student then communication may break down all together. You may see him get into difficulties and you may genuinely want to offer him your wisdom and experience but it will be rejected. He will be making short-term, emotionally driven decisions which your greater experience tells you will have long-term undesirable natural consequences but you will not be able to reach him in time.

The relationship building processes required to establish the emotional climate necessary for constantly increasing academic success take time. There are no quick-fix solutions. Building and repairing relationships, like all the most important things in life, takes time. Becoming impatient for results – as Covey puts it 'pulling up the flowers to see how the roots are doing' – simply throttles the goose in its prime.

Six key deposits you can make

Having and maintaining clear boundaries and expectations

Effective classroom leadership and relationships depend upon the establishment and maintenance of clear boundaries and expectations. Your students need to be clear about the boundaries that exist in your classroom. They need to know what behaviours will lead to social approval and academic success. The specific role of rules and routines in enabling you to establish clear boundaries and expectations is dealt with in Chapter 4.

Do not assume that your expectations, particularly regarding social behaviour, are so obvious that they do not need to be stated. An investment at the start of your relationship with your class in clarifying boundaries and expectations represents a major initial deposit in the emotional bank account of the whole class. It represents a great saving of time and effort further down the road and means that it is easy to keep this particular method of deposit topped up by continual approval when the boundaries are respected and expectations lived up to.

Paying attention to detail

It is often the little aspects of relationships that can make the biggest deposits or withdrawals. Take time with the little courtesies of relationships. A few examples are:

- Greeting each student by name within the first few minutes of every lesson.

- Holding doors open for your students when you can see they are struggling with a large bag.

- Not making a fuss when they haven't got a pen but lending them your own pen.

- Recognising when they don't feel too well and letting them sit quietly near a radiator.

- Remembering their birthday and wishing them a happy birthday as you call the register.

- Noticing when they come into school cold and wet and taking the time to allow them to warm up and dry their coats.

A small discourtesy, a little but significant sign of disrespect, can represent a major withdrawal from the bank account. You might choose to think of examples from your own relationships where a small act on behalf of another person has represented a major withdrawal from the bank account you have with them.

Treating students as individuals

By treating your students as individuals as well as members of the class you will be able to discover what, for them, constitutes a deposit in their emotional bank. Each of us responds to people's attempts to make deposits in our emotional deposit box in different ways. What for me constitutes a powerful deposit may for you be only a minor deposit.

Setting aside time to listen to what your students' concerns, hopes and fears are, even though they may not be directly related to the subject you are interested in teaching them, demonstrates an understanding of them as an individual that can constitute a large deposit. Recognising that there are human as well as academic agendas in play in your classroom gives you a powerful way to make regular deposits. However, a balance needs to be struck between addressing the human and academic agendas otherwise we lose the prime focus of our relationship and we will rapidly become overdrawn in other ways.

By taking the time to discover that Wayne has a pet snake and allowing him to talk to you about it and show you photographs of it, even showing interest in its well-being by having a brief chat in the corridor with him after he has had to take it to the vet, are all ways of making genuine deposits into his emotional box which will be directly transferable into every aspect of your teaching relationship.

Keeping your promises

You may not think that you make promises to your students and this may be true at an overt level, but there are many implied promises that we make simply through the relationship between teacher and student. Some examples of these implicit promises might be that:

- You promise to keep your students physically and psychologically safe.

- You promise to teach them in a way that enables them to learn most effectively.

- You promise to treat them with respect.

- You promise to enforce your classroom rules fairly and equitably.

- You promise to ensure that they can all enjoy their basic rights.

Breaking any of these implied promises represents a major withdrawal. Even if you do not break your promise towards a specific student, if they see you breaking it with one of their peers then they will not trust that you won't do the same to them. A breach of trust with one student, which other students either witness or become aware of, represents a major withdrawal from everybody's bank account.

Behaving with integrity

This goes beyond just keeping your promises. It means treating everybody with the same set of principles. It means both treating a student with respect and dignity in the classroom and not 'buying-in' to colleagues who, for whatever reason, run the student down in the staffroom. It means that you have to be clear about the values and principles that guide your decisions in the classroom and then 'walking the talk' in your everyday work with students.

If your students see you having 'favourites' in the classroom then you will be making major withdrawals from their account. This is not to say that you can't differentiate the behavioural curriculum in the classroom by varying the response you make to students' choices. Rather, it means that you need to base this variation upon your personal beliefs about the best way to help all of your students become winners.

Enabling your students to see on a day-to-day basis that you treat them all from the same, understandable and clear, principles, is opening the doors for some major emotional deposits in the classroom bank account.

Recognising, acknowledging and apologising for your mistakes

It is not just your students who will make some inappropriate choices from time to time. Because of the complex and vulnerable nature of human relationships, particularly in the strange world of the classroom, it is inevitable that you too will make some mistakes. You will misjudge a student's actions. You will misinterpret an action or a gesture. You will simply have a bad day. All of these can represent a sudden and major withdrawal.

By recognising, acknowledging and sincerely apologising when you make a mistake you will clearly demonstrate two things. Firstly, you are providing your students with a powerful role model for their future. People who are insecure in themselves, who are not empowered, find it difficult to make sincere apologies for their mistakes. Their feelings of self-worth are associated with the way others see them and an apology might threaten this opinion. By allowing students to see that you, a significant adult in their lives, have depth of self-confidence and personal security and by experiencing how much it puts into their emotional deposit boxes, you will be validating their efforts to develop true response-ability.

Secondly, you will be demonstrating that mistakes are part of the human condition. They are normal and natural – even you are capable of making them! Not only that, you will be demonstrating that you can recover from a mistake. It is not irredeemable. Again, you will be making a large deposit in all of your students' deposit boxes by demonstrating that they too can develop the confidence and skill to recover from their mistakes.

Key points

- Relationships are the key to academic achievement.

- We need to take care that we don't kill the goose simply because we are under pressure to produce more and more golden eggs.

- Winning classrooms have their prime focus upon building and maintaining relationships.

- You can consider the classroom emotional climate as a bank account. You must make deposits before you can make a withdrawal.

- Going overdrawn in your account with students always has negative repercussions.

- Deposits dwindle with time and need to be constantly replaced.

- There are six key ways of making deposits into your classroom bank account:

  - Having and maintaining clear boundaries and expectations

  - Paying attention to detail

  - Treating students as individuals

  - Keeping your promises

  - Behaving with integrity

  - Recognising, acknowledging and apologising for your mistakes.

Activity 5.1

Review the 'Six key deposits you can make' section in this chapter. Under each of the headings list up to five actions that you can take on a regular basis to make deposits in your students' emotional deposit boxes.

Having and maintaining clear boundaries and expectations

1. _____

2. _____

3. _____

4. _____

5. _____

Paying attention to detail

1. _____

2. _____

3. _____

4. _____

5. _____

Treating students as individuals

1. _____

2. _____

3. _____

4. _____

5. _____

Activity 5.1 – continued

Keeping your promises

1. _____

2. _____

3. _____

4. _____

5. _____

Behaving with integrity

1. _____

2. _____

3. _____

4. _____

5. _____

Recognising, acknowledging and apologising for your mistakes

1. _____

2. _____

3. _____

4. _____

5. _____

Proactive response

This next part will be extremely tough but the rewards are often tremendous even in a short period of time.

For the next two weeks keep a mental diary of how often you manage to make these deposits.

Alongside this, every time you make a withdrawal from your emotional deposit accounts try to find an opportunity to replace the withdrawal.

Questions for professional development

What do you feel about the topics covered in this chapter?

What are some of the implications of the topics within your classroom?

What is it most important to you to remember from this chapter?

Chapter 6

MOTIVATION

We can Rodney... You can do anything if you want it hard enough. We can do it Rodney, we can do it!
        Del Trotter – Only Fools and Horses – 'Cash and Curry'

How can you make Mary learn?

The simple answer is, *you can't*!

Nobody can *make* Mary, or anybody else for that matter, learn.

Equally, there is no such thing as a demotivated student.

- Watch them playing the 'mating game' in a nightclub!

- Watch them as they get themselves out of bed early on a Saturday morning to spend the day packing shelves in the supermarket!

- Watch them tidying their bedroom because they won't be allowed out until they do!

- Watch them avoid working in your classroom!

They certainly aren't demotivated then!

All of these examples give us the evidence that our students can show highly motivated behaviour *if the circumstances are right*.

We can't make Mary learn. We *can* attempt to vary the learning environment in such a way that she will be encouraged to do something that will result in her learning.

There are many things in Mary's life that we can't do anything about. We can't change her family, her physical appearance, where she lives, or the number of brothers and sisters that she has. However, there are many things that we can change or vary about Mary's circumstances that may encourage her to learn.

It is these 'variables' that can provide us with the key to unlock the door for Mary's learning.

The work that we set, the way we interact with her, the classroom environment, where she is seated, the rewards and sanctions that we apply as consequences to the choices she makes are all variables that are, usually speaking, within our control. If our goal is to create a winning environment for our students, then our skill in managing and balancing these variables will largely determine the extent to which we achieve our goal. Several of these variables, in particular the factors affecting empowerment, are so essential that we have devoted an entire chapter to them. What we are concerned with in this chapter is the concept of motivation itself.

What is motivation?

Motivation can be defined as *a state of need or desire that results in a person becoming activated to do something*. Motivation results from an unsatisfied need. We cannot make our students learn – what we can achieve is a manipulation of their environment (physical and psychological) in such a way that they *might* become more motivated. In Chapter 3 we talked about the gap between our self-image and our ideal self. If there is no gap we get complacency. If the gap is too big we get demotivation with consequent opt-out and ICB behaviours. Effective classroom leaders are skilled at creating a gap that the pupil can both envisage being able to cross and see some benefit in achieving.

Understanding motivational 'house style'

The public perception of the 'motivated person' is someone who sets and achieves goals in their lives. Indeed, these are the students who we most value in schools. They are the students who 'buy into' the targets we set for them and direct their behaviour towards achieving our motivational goals. They respond to our positive feedback and work hard to achieve the rewarding carrots we dangle in front of them. Many of them will simply work hard because their teachers are highly skilled at making frequent payments into their emotional 'deposit box' (see Chapter 5). There is no doubt about it: they are a joy to teach. Much of these students' motivation comes from a desire to please us and, because of this, they can leave us with the feeling that teaching is a worthwhile profession after all!

If only all of our students were this highly motivated!

The cruel truth is that they are!

They are just not motivated *towards* the targets, goals and rewards that we offer them. Before we go on to examine the range of motivational variables that we might consider managing within our classrooms there is another, and highly significant, factor that we need to consider – the normal or preferred *direction* of each of our students' motivation.

The best way to understand this is to consider the following situation:

A teacher has worked very hard to introduce a positive, rewards based system within their classroom. They have a wide variety of rewards on offer from simple, but immensely powerful, examples of social approval such as smiles, nods and thumbs up through to the more tangible feedback systems such as notes home, certificates and photographs. For many of her pupils this is working well. Many of her students value the rewards on offer and will either continue to make positive choices about their behaviour or modify their behaviour to gain them. In fact, by using high frequency methods of giving social approval, she is constantly reinforcing her students' motivational desire to please her. These students are motivated *towards* the rewards she is using. Also, at the same time as providing powerful, motivational rewards, she is regularly able to make valuable payments into her students' deposit boxes. The motivational spiral is upwards.

However, there are a significant minority of her students for whom these rewards seem to have no effect. They seem to be gaining nothing from their behaviour apart from short-term satisfaction and transient peer recognition. No amount of positive recognition seems to be effective. One day she arrives in school feeling tired and dejected. In particular she is feeling downcast about the prospects of facing another day making the supreme effort to be positive with a group of students who reject every 'motivational' advance. Her special concern is about Martin. He doesn't seem to respond to any form of reward system. His satisfaction seems to stem from seeing other members of the class upset by his behaviour. She has tried a whole range of positive rewards in an attempt to build upon the times when he is behaving appropriately towards other students – all to no avail.

As she goes into the class, Martin is provoking Samantha again. Something wells up inside her and it overrides her professional, 'positive is always best' approach. Calmly but assertively she addresses Martin and sets out the consequence of continued unacceptable behaviour. 'Martin, I'm not putting up with this behaviour any longer and neither is Samantha. If you continue to choose to talk to Samantha that way you'll be choosing to stay in at lunchtime.' She blocks Martin's objections and his attempts to deny that he was on the same planet at the time of the incident. She leaves him in no doubt that she really 'means business' and he will have to face what, to him, is an unacceptable consequence – Martin loves playing football at lunchtimes – if he chooses to continue the behaviour. To her surprise, Martin starts making more positive choices about his behaviour. She smiles and recognises his new, improved choices. Martin smiles back!

Thinking about it overnight she realises that Martin's change in attitude is because he is an '*away*' motivator. Martin's preferred motivational style is to move away from what he perceives as a consequence he wishes to avoid rather than 'towards' a goal he wants to achieve. As she enters the classroom Martin runs up to her and says 'Can I go out to play at lunchtime today?' She smiles. 'If you make the same good choices that you made yesterday, of course you can Martin.' His continued good choices mean that she can continue to give Martin the positive social recognition that he needs in order for her to start to come into surplus in Martin's emotional deposit box. She has found the key to developing the sort of positive relationship that will eventually mean he doesn't have to torment other pupils in order to feel good about himself.

In terms of the way we become motivated, as with many other aspects of our behaviour, we all have a 'house style'.

What is your normal, 'house style' of motivation? (This is not a scientifically validated test!)

Which of these situations best describes your normal behaviour?

- **When you are sitting at a table marking a pile of books do you set yourself a target of marking another ten books and then getting yourself a cup of coffee? (Towards your motivational goal of a cup of coffee.) Alternatively, do you plough on with the marking until you become uncomfortably thirsty and your back aches from sitting too long before you take a break? (Away from the discomfort.)**

- **Do you tend to choose friends who challenge and stimulate you? (Towards new goals and experiences.) Alternatively, do you tend to choose friends with whom you feel comfortable and who do not challenge you? (Away from challenge.)**

- **Does your sense of satisfaction increase as you move closer towards goals and targets you have set for yourself? (Towards – goal-orientated behaviour.) Alternatively, does your enthusiasm for projects tend to wane as the pressure to get things done diminishes? (Away – discomfort avoidance behaviour.)**

We are all capable of displaying both towards as well as away-from motivational styles. It is simply that we all have, to a greater or lesser extent, a preferred style. Nor is it necessarily that one style is 'better' than the other. There are, however, some problems for people who are habitual away-from motivators:

- Their motivation tends to be cyclic. It is high when they are close to the cause of the discomfort they are trying to avoid and drops the further from it they get. Quite often, away-from motivators will seemingly cause minor crises in their lives simply to keep themselves motivated!

- Many away-from motivators can, if they are not careful, suffer from quite high levels of stress. They need to play a very careful game of allowing the tension to build to the point where they will become sufficiently motivated without it building so far that they start to display opt-out or ICB behaviours.

Dancing the delicate dance

There is no doubt that positive goal setting coupled with both positive social feedback and tangible symbols of success should be our preferred option for providing motivation in our classrooms. It builds positive relationships by enabling you to constantly make deposits in the emotional bank account between you and the student.

However, occasionally you will come across a student for whom these strategies seem to have little effect. They only seem to make positive choices about their behaviour when they think something undesirable will result if they continue to make negative choices.

This is where you need to dig deep into your resources as a classroom leader. You will need to 'dance the delicate dance' in order to help this student become a winner.

In order to help them become motivated towards more positive choices you will need to provide some form of meaningful disincentive for any inappropriate choices they make. If you get the disincentive wrong by making it too significant you run the risk of making large withdrawals from the bank account. You run the risk of causing the student to give up even more with a consequent deleterious effect upon their behaviour. Equally, in order to build a more positive self-image and reduce the need for the negative choices, alongside consistent application of the appropriate disincentive, you will need to constantly provide meaningful and genuine positive social feedback for the new positive choices the student is making. In fact, you will consciously have to provide more positive emotional deposits in this particular student's bank account in order to compensate for the continued need to make withdrawals.

This is probably the most sophisticated demonstration of the art of 'tough care' that we examined in *Confident Classroom Leadership*. It is easy, with a student who rejects our positive advances, to overdo the 'tough' and apply sanctions that simply put us into negative emotional equity with the student and therefore make the behaviours worse. Equally, it is easy to overdo the 'care' to the extent where we never match our pupils' motivational style by applying clear and meaningful disincentives for negative choices. The skill of the effective classroom leader lies in achieving a balance between enabling students to become motivated towards making positive choices and, particularly for those students who need disincentives to help them become motivated, constantly giving out messages that say you care about them as people.

Variables

So far we have discussed the notion that to create a motivational, winning classroom environment you need to use your skills to manage those variables that are within your control. Also, we need to recognise that not all of our students fit into the classic pattern of the goal-orientated motivator.

We will now look in some detail at the range of variables that it may well be within your ability to manage.

The first set of variables are those related to the student's feelings and are:

- The degree of tension or concern that exists within the learner.

- The degree to which the student feels the experience is pleasant, unpleasant or neutral.

The second set of variables relate to the student's degree of:

- Interest in the task.

- Feelings of personal success.

- Perceived task difficulty.

- Interest in feedback.

- Relationship between the activity and an internalised goal.

None of these variables will operate in isolation. Humans are complex beings and many variables will come into play at any one time. They will be considered one at a time below, but in reality we may be working with several variables at any one time.

Examples of manageable variables

1. The degree of tension or concern

No tension or concern results in no motivation. Consider this example:

You are sitting on a beautiful beach relaxing under a comfortably warm sun. A gentle breeze and the peaceful lapping of the waves add to the tranquillity. You have nothing that you need to get on with and your time is genuinely your own. What will you be motivated to do? Probably nothing!

There is one fly in the ointment! You have forgotten to turn off your mobile phone. When it rings you pick it up and the caller tells you that you need to read through the papers that have just been delivered to your hotel. What will you do? You may decide to go back and read them now, or you might resolve to read them later, or ignore the call altogether.

A few minutes later you receive another message. This time you are told that when you return to work the next day you will be tested on the contents of the paper. How much will your motivation increase? Enough to stir yourself from your chair? Will you put the reading off to the last minute? Will you still resolve to refuse to read the papers at all and (expletive deleted) the consequences?

A third message informs you that the results of this test will be posted on the school website. What effect will this have on your state? You may still resolve to resist the task but your emotional state may not be as comfortable as before. The chances are that you will, albeit reluctantly, get on with the task.

A fourth and final message informs you that unless you get a score of at least 95% on the test your job will be in jeopardy. Almost certainly, you will give up the rest and recuperation and be half way through the papers before the end of the message! Unfortunately, because of the increased pressure, it is now difficult to concentrate upon your reading. Your mind keeps dwelling upon the unfairness of the pressure you have been put under. Perhaps the feelings of resentment will have increased to the point where you slam the papers down in disgust shouting to anybody that wants to listen 'OK. If that's the way you want it, go ahead and sack me!'

This little scenario demonstrates an important concept about motivation and tension. Tension can either come in the form of your desire to achieve a goal (towards) or your need to avoid discomfort (away) but in either case, no tension – no motivation!

Motivation, then, increases as the tension increases up to a certain point. When the tension increases too much the student will begin to have to use some of their emotional energy to deal with the tension itself. Ultimately, the tension may increase so much that they give up altogether.

This is the skill of the teacher. Matching the level of tension to the learner is a high level skill.

For some students we need to add a 'cost' or imposed away-from tension to their choice not to take part in the learning experience. Frequently simply stating that if the student chooses not to complete the work in the allotted time they will be choosing to do it in their own time will be successful. The skill lies in providing a level of tension that will result in goal achievement without tipping the student over into a state of tension avoidance.

Conversely, we may come across a student whose lack of motivation stems from too much tension. This can frequently arise as a result of unrealistic demands from home or overly severe costs imposed by teachers for non-compliance. If, for instance, a parent constantly expect levels of achievement that the student does not believe they are capable of attaining then they will become demotivated. Alongside working with the parents to reduce the tension they are applying, we will need to break the student's tasks down into small, achievable steps in order to help them begin to believe they are capable of success.

2. *The degree to which the student feels the experience is pleasant, unpleasant or neutral*

Pleasant feelings will increase motivation. Unpleasant feelings will increase motivation but to a lesser level – often with undesirable side effects. Neutral feelings will have no effect upon motivation.

Public celebrations of success – work displayed on walls, putting test scores on notice boards, public recognition of achievement in assemblies, etc. – can frequently prove to be a great motivator for a wide variety of students. They will be particularly powerful if we find ways of giving equal recognition to a wide range of achievements – both social and academic – as a means of celebrating the range of difference within our school community. Activities in which students are enabled to feel positive about themselves as people and to have those positive feelings endorsed by significant others can be extremely motivating.

Making Michael feel good about a well-presented piece of work will motivate him. Equally, making Michael feel bad about a poorly presented piece of work may also motivate him – providing that we are in surplus in our emotional account with Michael and therefore don't make him feel so bad that it isn't worth trying again.

Simply letting him be will do nothing to motivate him.

Again, there will be some students for whom these public celebrations will not be motivational. In fact, for some who have poor or damaged self-images public celebrations may be de-motivational. They have learned to get their feelings of success from their lack of involvement. For these students we might consider introducing some 'cost' to a lack of participation in learning. For a student who is not interested in how well they did on the last maths test and therefore scored poorly, we might introduce additional maths coaching at a time when their peers are taking part in enjoyable social activities. But again, care needs to be given to these sorts of strategies. If the student feels that we are simply punishing them rather than using a supportive consequence the resultant withdrawal may be too high.

3. *Interest in the task*

Interest is probably the task variable that is most easily manipulated by teachers.

Having knowledge of your students' hopes, desires and interests is essential to developing motivated students. Teachers who seem to be most successful at motivating their students always seem to be those that find it easiest to match the task to the interests of their students. They can interpret what they want to teach in a way that enables their students to easily hook into it.

Tasks that link to your students' interests will not only result in an increased desire for task success but will enable them to embed the learning into a broader context thus making it easier to both recall and utilise it in a wider range of areas.

All of us will be more motivated towards the achievement of a task if we can determine the 'What's in it for me?' – WIIFM – factor. While altruism is a highly desirable characteristic it is still frequently associated with a WIIFM – I feel good when I see others enjoying themselves.

4. *Feelings of personal success related to task difficulty*

Success and interest are inextricably linked. We are more likely to be interested in a task if we think we are likely to be successful and, in turn, we are more likely to be successful if we are interested in the task.

While not being synonymous, degree of difficulty is frequently directly related to feelings of success. You will probably be getting very little feeling of success from reading these words. You are a competent reader and therefore the simple act of decoding this print will have little effect upon your feelings of success. However, for a six year old or somebody just learning English, there can be much pleasure to be had from the simple act of decoding. Again, the line we tread is fine. Increase the difficulty level too far (give this document to an average five year old and make it important that she reads it) and you will create a state of severe demotivation.

Breaking tasks down into small achievable steps can be a strategy for building success with students but only if achieving each step represents a sufficient level of difficulty. Step achievement must provide the student with genuine feelings of success without slipping into demotivation either through too much pressure or through boredom.

5. Interest in feedback

Imagine how difficult it would be to try to teach students without ever being able to find out if what you were doing was being effective. Engagement in tasks without the opportunity for feedback rapidly becomes pointless and consequently demotivating.

The more specific the feedback, the more motivating it is likely to be. Consider these two statements:

'Well done, that was a reasonably good shot.'

'Well done. That was a good attempt. You were just a touch too high and a bit too much to the left.'

Which would leave you feeling more confident about taking your second shot?

Praise is important. We all need to be told 'Well done' or 'Good job, thanks' but praise linked to specific information is motivational.

Giving specific, verifiable and preferably factual information as part of your feedback is essential. You need to be alert to the need to pay at least as much attention to the points that contributed to success as you do to pointing out errors. Which of these do you think is most likely to set the student off in a positive frame of mind?

'You need to make sure that you label the axis on the graph next time.'

or,

'Well done. You have chosen the right scale on your graph, clearly marked all the points and joined them up with a smooth curve. To make the next one even better, try to remember to label the axis clearly.'

6. Relationship between the activity and an internalised goal

This is about the difference between intrinsic and extrinsic motivation. Reading a book because you enjoy the process of reading and get pleasure from engaging in the information you are receiving is an example of intrinsic motivation. Doing your reading homework because you know the teacher will give you a merit mark if you do is about extrinsic motivation. They both represent a 'towards' motivational style but they are towards very different goals.

We can all recall teachers who had perfect control over their students' behaviour while they were in the class but chaos ensued as soon as they left the room. Again, the students were responding to extrinsic motivation – keeping the teacher happy – while she was in the room. However, as soon as she left, other, intrinsic, motivational factors took over – the need to have a good time!

The 'stick and carrot' approach is the classic example of extrinsic motivation. It can be, and often is, highly effective in stimulating students to move towards the teacher's learning goals. However there is a downside. Overuse of the stick approach frequently results in regular and large withdrawals from the emotional bank account. It quickly becomes depleted or moves into deficit. The students rapidly becoming adept at *stick avoidance* behaviours rather than focused upon appropriate learning behaviours.

Conversely, overuse of the carrot approach can result in the need to find more and more carrots. Alternatively, the students may get fed up with carrots altogether and we have to find an equally motivating substitute!

Extrinsic motivation should be seen as one powerful step on the path towards developing intrinsic motivation. If we can connect the learning goal with the students' needs, desires or interests then we will begin to develop intrinsic motivation. Learning success will enable the students to achieve their personal goals and will become self-sustaining.

This is one reason why teaching spelling is so hard with some pupils. The justification we often give to students for going through the stress of learning to write is to be able communicate via the written word. If your students get no intrinsic motivation from the simple fact of writing or, if they get no sense of satisfaction from your pleasure in telling them they have finished a good piece of writing, then they can make no direct connection between the act – spelling – and the eventual goal – communication. Thair iz knot aktualee a direkt reelayshonship iz thair? So hou kan U mowtivayt them 2 lern 2 spel?

Specific strategies for increasing motivation

Eric Jensen (see Recommended reading and additional resources) has identified several key motivators throughout his work. We believe the most important in terms of the work outlined in this book are:

- **Give learners control and choice**

  Students need to be allowed to control, at various times, how, when and with whom they learn a topic. Control and choice give the student a chance to express and feel valued. Allowing control and choice will lower stress levels and enable teachers to better establish what the student really wants to do and learn.

- **Positive social bonding**

  Students will perform and learn better within an atmosphere where positive social bonding is established. As was indicated in the section on trust deficits, students are more motivated when they can trust that the teacher has their best interests at heart. Motivation is also increased when teachers encourage students to work together in groups or teams. The sense of interdependence reduces feelings of helplessness and stress.

- **What's In It For Them (WIIFM)**

  Our brains are primarily geared to survival. We will learn what we believe we need to learn in order to have our immediate needs met. If your students need what you are offering they will learn it. Also, the more closely the context relates to the students' personal lives the more likely they are to be interested. A young (5 to 6 year old) student's needs will be focused upon security, predictability and social acceptance. By 14, they have probably moved to peer acceptance and approval, a sense of self and hope. By 18, they will be more interested in autonomy and independence. We need to use what is appropriate for the age and maturity of the students we are working with.

- **Low stress – High challenge**

  As we showed in Chapter 3, in situations where students feel they are likely to be unsuccessful, their stress levels will rise. This, in turn, will inhibit their ability to learn effectively. Students will learn best when they do not feel threatened by failure but are given tasks that challenge their abilities and resources.

- **Safety**

  We have dealt with psychological safety at length elsewhere, but attention also needs to be paid to students' physical safety. They need to feel that they are protected from physical danger (from either objects or other students) as well as having their needs for adequate lighting, water, food, movement and seating met.

- **Hope**

  Students need to know that it is possible for them to succeed. A sense of hope is essential. No matter how far behind the others we are or what obstacles remain to be overcome, hope will keep us moving on. All television game shows rely upon giving all participants hope of success no matter how far behind the leaders they are. This is what stops them giving up and leaving the studio.

- **Frequency of feedback**

  Every student needs to get feedback, from the teacher or peers, at the very least every 30 minutes. The single most effective (legal) stimulant for the brain is information. Immediate and dramatic information will stimulate the brain more effectively than anything else. Look at video games and fruit machines. They both give high frequency and dramatic feedback. The feedback motivates you to keep playing.

The ignoble art of demotivation!

Consider the following approaches that have a proven 'track record' as highly successful strategies for bringing about a state of demotivation – many of them will also work with adults as well as students:

- Ignore any improvements.

- Punish any failure swiftly and harshly.

- Don't listen to their opinions.

- Ridicule any errors – preferably publicly.

- If you do ask for opinions, ignore their response.

- Disregard any good results on the grounds that 'They should be doing that anyway'.

- Expect students to be intrinsically motivated simply because you were when you were at school.

- Don't provide any support or guidance.

- Refuse to be interested in them as people.

- Have lots of petty rules and religiously enforce them.

- Have unrealistically high expectations.

- Have boringly low expectations.

- Refuse to accept that you are paid to work with any but the most motivated students.

Have you got any more clues about ways of motivating your students?

Key points

- You can't make students learn.

- There are many factors that contribute to the student's state over which you have little or no control.

- The good news is that there are many factors over which you have direct control.

- Developing motivation in the demotivated is about the manipulation of a variety of factors. These factors are usually associated with feelings of belonging, self-worth, security and emotional stimulation.

- We need to be aware that for some, away-from motivated students, we need to be especially skilful in 'dancing the delicate dance'.

- The skilful teacher manipulates the students' learning environment in such a way as to match the strategy they have chosen to the hopes, desires and interests of their students.

- The most powerful factor to develop is intrinsic motivation. Connecting the learning environment with the students' internal goals will develop sustained motivation.

- 'Scatter gun' approaches to motivation are rarely successful with the hard-to-motivate. Many of the strategies need to be carefully matched to the individual students. What can prove motivating for one student can result in avoidance behaviours in others.

- Motivated students arise from the skill and professionalism of the staff concerned.

- Avoiding demotivating our students requires almost as much skill as proactively motivating them.

Questions for professional development

What do you feel about the topics covered in this chapter?

What are some of the implications of the topics within your classroom?

What is it most important to you to remember from this chapter?

Chapter 7

SOME PRACTICAL OPPORTUNITIES FOR INTERVENTION

Clearly, for humanistic reasons as well as performance ones, it is time to incorporate emotional intelligence into your programme.

Karen Stone McCown *et al.*

Introduction

With the constant pressure for more and tighter targets, with greater pressure for results, it is only to be expected that teachers will acknowledge the need to work within an emotional curriculum but their 'gut' reaction will frequently be – 'I'm working at 110 per cent capacity at the moment. I haven't got the time to fit in anything else no matter how beneficial it looks. There's no slack left any more!' – and we quite agree.

Throughout this book we have tried to show ways that you can incorporate the ideas into your everyday practice without having to find any extra time. For instance, all of the ideas included in Chapter 5 concerning payments into and withdrawals from your classroom's 'bank account' simply require a change in attitude and emphasis rather than any additional teaching time.

However, there is one key aspect of developing emotional literacy in classrooms that has recently become a key feature of our work with schools and that, at first, did seem to require additional curriculum time. This aspect was the proactive teaching of the language of emotion (see below). However, we are extremely fortunate that we are working with a group of highly talented and creative teachers who are constantly seeking out ways of teaching this key aspect from within their current curriculum rather than in addition to it.

Why teach the language of emotion?

When we began to look at the way students, particularly those who seemed to find it most difficult to cope in schools, responded at an emotional level, we noticed something quite remarkable. They did not seem to have a sophisticated language for talking about their emotions. In fact they had a very restricted emotional vocabulary. They were either 'OK' or 'mad' with somebody. They were either 'all right' or 'happy'. There were no points in between. This was also reflected in their physical expression of emotion. Their physical response to being slightly jostled in the corridor was the same as if they had just been assaulted – there was no gradation. When we began to investigate further, this correlation between a restricted emotional vocabulary and a lack of gradation in emotional expression seemed to hold true throughout the age range.

We decided to take our own advice and try a proactive response. What would happen if we actively taught students a more sophisticated linguistic repertoire and proactively discussed gradated emotional responses? To our delight, our working hypothesis seems, so far, to have been proven to be true. The more sophisticated the students' emotional language becomes, the more we find opportunities to show them a range of emotional responses, the more they are able to gradate their own emotional responses. Equally delightfully, the effect seems to be true throughout the Key Stages.

Teaching the language of emotion

Obviously, in a book of this size we haven't got the space to go into detail about the whole range of opportunities that the teachers we are working with have found to teach gradated emotional responses. Rather, what we have included is a range of ideas that may both whet your appetite to experiment in your own classroom and show you how these concepts can be incorporated in a way that enables you to work smarter not harder.

For obvious reasons, we have not included Circle Time and PSHE as these represent our more formal opportunities for discussion. What is crucial is that these sorts of activity are not confined to set areas of the timetable – 'It's Thursday morning so it must be emotional literacy!' – but should be embedded in as many aspects as possible. In this way the skills become part of our students' everyday experiences.

Examples from within the curriculum

Key Stages 1 and 2

1. Literacy hour

Using the discussion about characters in books to focus upon emotional response by asking questions such as:

> How do you think Little Bear would feel about that?
>
> Would he be very scared or just a little bit scared?
>
> Can you think of other times when you were a little bit scared?
>
> Can you think of times when you were very scared?

With older students there are opportunities to explore the social use of language. These provide a golden opportunity for exploring a thesaurus to examine the range of expressions used for particular emotional situations.

For instance:

HAPPY: glad, contented, fortunate, gratified, cheerful, joyful, alive, pleased, lively, delighted, high, up.

One of the teachers we are working with (Y3) has her 'word of the week' displayed at the front of the room and students win points for their team for every opportunity they can find to bring it appropriately into conversation. The last time we were in her room the word was 'disheartened'!

2. Art

Using creative ways of drawing gradated emotions.

When discussing various artists students can share their emotional responses to discover what range of response there is in the class.

3. History

Alongside discussing actual events, opportunities can be made to discuss the way various historical characters may have responded.

> When Henry found out that Thomas had been murdered how do you think he might have felt?
>
> What sorts of feelings might he have had?
>
> How would the Knights have felt when they first did it? How would their emotions have changed later?

4. Maths

When looking at the use of data, the class can gather data about the range of emotional responses to adverts, news events, etc.

These can then be displayed on the classroom wall as a visual representation of gradated emotional response.

Key Stages 3 and 4

There are obvious opportunities, which can be located in assemblies, PSE and individual discussions with students about their work and their behaviour. Almost all of the examples from Key Stages 1 and 2 can be translated for older students. Some additional examples might be:

1. Science

In studying the brain, incorporate the different functions of the reptilian, limbic and neo-cortex and how they affect emotional response.

Making predictions of outcomes in experiments can involve brief discussions about how the students felt about taking a risk. Did the notion of failure generate a different response to the idea of making a mistake?

Famous scientists/inventors like Edison demonstrated persistence and motivation.

What would be the differing emotional responses of an oil company executive to Greenpeace occupying a platform to prevent dumping?

2. Physical Education

In discussing motivation for winning or just participation you can calibrate levels of motivation.

Discussing the notion of a 'noble' or calm loser by exploring what internal dialogue they may have had to remain calm.

Using metaphor or analogy to assist emotional problem-solving, e.g. Michelle trips over a lace during a race on Sports day. She really wanted to win the race. Brainstorm her feelings. Why when she got up might she have smiled to her friends and said 'It doesn't matter'.

3. MFL

Exploring the different ways in which emotion is accompanied by non-verbal cues in the relevant target language.

Develop specific modules in which students are encouraged to describe their emotions in target language.

Devise questionnaires for imaginary or real pen-pals that elicit gradated responses about their interests and hobbies.

4. Technology

Teaching the vocabulary of evaluating design beyond the 'It's good', 'It's rubbish!'

General classroom opportunities

1. When talking to students about their work or behaviour there is a wealth of opportunity for you to display your own gradated emotional response to your students' work:

   'I'm very pleased with the way you are choosing to work today.'

   'I am a little bit upset by the way you chose to talk to Shaquib just now.'

   'I'm getting a little frustrated by the noise level at this table.'

2. Inviting the students to suggest why you are 'very' rather than 'a little bit' pleased or 'a little bit upset' rather than 'very upset' can follow either of these sorts of statements.

3. When calling the register you can ask your students to answer their name followed by how they are feeling today.

   If they give a bland response such as 'OK' you can follow it with 'A little bit OK, or a lot OK?'

4. Try to develop a gradated language for all of your emotional responses. Make sure that everything is not simply 'very good' or 'silly'. A thesaurus can be a great boon here too.

5. With early years students (and those who are emotionally very immature) the 'P' Levels provide a wealth of prompts for teaching gradated emotional responses.

Questions for professional development

What do you feel about the topics covered in this chapter?

What are some of the implications of the topics within your classroom?

What is it most important to you to remember from this chapter?

REFERENCES

Boyd, B. (1997) 'How we lift our pupils' game in 100 days', *Times Educational Supplement*, 23 May.

Canfield, J. and Siccone, F. (1995) *101 Ways to develop student self-esteem and responsibility*. Massachusetts: Allyn & Bacon.

Covey, S. (1989) *The Seven Habits of Highly Effective People*. London: Simon & Schuster.

Glasser, W. (1990) *The Quality School: Managing Students without Coercion*. New York: HarperCollins.

Goleman, D. (1996) *Emotional Intelligence*. London: Bloomsbury Publishing.

Hook, P. and Vass, A. (1999) *Confident Classroom Leadership*. London: David Fulton Publishers.

Hughes, M. (1999) *Closing the Learning Gap*. Stafford: Network Educational Press.

Jensen, E. (1995) *Super Teaching*. California: Turning Point Publishing.

Robbins, A. (1988) *Unlimited Power*. London: Simon & Schuster.

Salovey, P. and Mayer, J. (1989) 'Emotional Intelligence', *Imagination, Cognition and Personality*, v. 9.

Stone McCown, K. *et al.* (1988) *Self Science*. Santa Monica: Six Seconds Publishing.

RECOMMENDED READING AND ADDITIONAL RESOURCES

Confident Classroom Leadership, P. Hook and A. Vass. London: David Fulton Publishers.

Closing the Learning Gap, M.   ss.

How to raise a child with a hig

The Intelligent School, B. Mac

The Seven Habits of Highly Ef   chuster.

Self Science, K. Stone McCov   ng.

Friendly Kids, Friendly Classr   Longmans.

The Learning Revolution, G. I   Learning Systems.

The Art of Teaching Peacefull   lishers.

Super Teaching, E. Jensen. C

DATE DUE		

GAYLORD   #3523PI   Printed in USA